T0304695

POLICE
PROCEDURE AND
EVIDENCE IN THE
CRIMINAL
JUSTICE SYSTEM

POLICE PROCEDURE AND EVIDENCE IN THE CRIMINAL JUSTICE SYSTEM

THE PROFESSIONAL POLICING CURRICULUM IN PRACTICE

Routledge
Taylor & Francis Group

LONDON AND NEW YORK

BARRIE ARCHER AND GEORGE ELLISON
SERIES EDITOR: TONY BLOCKLEY

First published in 2023 by Critical Publishing Ltd

Published 2025 by Routledge
4 Park Square, Milton Park, Abingdon, Oxon OX14 4RN
605 Third Avenue, New York, NY 10017

Routledge is an imprint of the Taylor & Francis Group, an informa business

British Library Cataloguing in Publication Data
A CIP record for this book is available from the British Library

ISBN: 9781041056416 (hbk)
ISBN: 9781914171987 (pbk)
ISBN: 9781041056409 (ebk)

Cover and text design by Out of House Limited

DOI: 10.4324/9781041056409

CONTENTS

ABOUT THE SERIES EDITOR

TONY BLOCKLEY

Tony Blockley is the lead for policing at Leeds Trinity University, responsible for co-ordinating policing higher education, including developing programmes and enhancing the current provision in line with the Police Education Qualification Framework (PEQF) and supporting the College of Policing. He served within policing for over 30 years, including a role as Chief Superintendent and Head of Crime.

ABOUT THE AUTHORS

BARRIE ARCHER

Barrie Archer is a lecturer in policing at the University of Derby. He specialises in delivering the police constable degree apprenticeship (PCDA) module, drawing on his experience as an officer with Warwickshire Police and his legal qualifications.

GEORGE ELLISON

George Ellison is a senior lecturer in law at the University of Derby, working both within the law school and on the police degree programme. He served with Merseyside Police for 33 years in several departments, and is a qualified barrister.

FOREWORD

Police professionalism has seen significant developments over recent years, including the implementation of the Vision 2025 and the establishment of the Police Education Qualification Framework (PEQF). There is no doubt that policing has become complex, and that complexity and associated challenges increase day by day with greater scrutiny, expectations and accountability. The educational component of police training and development therefore allows officers to gain a greater understanding and appreciation of the theories and activities associated with high-quality policing provision.

The scholastic element of the Vision 2025 provides an opportunity to engage in meaningful insight and debate around some of the most sensitive areas of policing while also applying the lessons of the past to develop the service for the future. While there are many books and articles on numerous subjects associated with policing, this new series – *The Professional Policing Curriculum in Practice* – provides an insightful opportunity to start that journey. It distils the key concepts and topics within policing into an accessible format, combining theory and practice to provide you with a secure basis of knowledge and understanding.

With policing now a degree-level-entry profession, this has provided a unique opportunity to develop fully up-to-date books for student and trainee police officers that focus on the content of the PEQF curriculum, are tailored specifically to the new pre-join routes, and reflect the diversity and complexity of twenty-first-century society. Each book is stand-alone, but they also work together to layer information as you progress through your programme. The pedagogical features of the books have been carefully designed to improve your understanding and critical thinking skills within the context of policing. They include learning objectives, case studies, evidence-based practice examples, critical thinking and reflective activities, and summaries of key concepts. Each chapter also includes a guide to further reading, meaning you don't have to spend hours researching to find that piece of information you are looking for.

The criminal justice system is a series of complex processes that can be challenging, but also have a significant impact on the external views of justice. This complexity raises many pitfalls that have significant repercussions for the criminal justice system and, in particular, victims, witnesses and defendants.

This book examines police procedure and evidence within the context of the criminal justice system. It explores the complex processes and some of the many challenges involved. There is a particular need for policing students and police officers to have an understanding of this topic because there is a clear requirement to understand the links between police procedures and the use of evidence within the criminal justice system. Ultimately, this understanding will ensure fairness and justice within the system.

Having been involved in policing for over 40 years, the benefits of these books are obvious to me: I see them becoming the go-to guides for the PEQF curriculum across all the various programmes associated with the framework, while also having relevance for more experienced officers.

Tony Blockley
Discipline Head: Policing
Leeds Trinity University

CHAPTER 1
POLICE POWERS

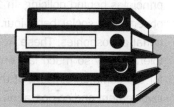

LEARNING OBJECTIVES

AFTER READING THIS CHAPTER YOU WILL BE ABLE TO:

* recognise the Peelian principles;

* understand how the Peelian principles are applicable to modern-day policing;

* understand how police powers and policing interact with each other;

* comprehend the use of various police powers.

INTRODUCTION

This chapter discusses the powers available to police officers and how they have developed since the introduction of the Metropolitan Police Act 1829, which established the Metropolitan Police (the Met). While this was not the first recognised police force – that honour falls to Scotland – it is recognised as the birth of modern policing.

No discussion on police powers can start without an understanding of the origin of the principles behind policing. In 1829, Sir Robert Peel, the then Home Secretary and a keen observer of social behaviour, established the Metropolitan Police with several foundational philosophies. These were based on the acceptance and realisation that the public tolerate only so much law enforcement and to present a police force there was a need for the common consent of the public. Further to this, there was a realisation that public involvement and co-operation were necessary for law enforcement to be successful. These foundational principles form the bedrock of policing. It has long been argued by a number of academics that the Peelian principles are simply a twentieth-century creation and that others are responsible for creating the principles, namely the first commissioners of the Met, Lieutenant-Colonel Sir Charles Rowan (c 1782–1852, commissioner 1829–50) and barrister Richard Mayne (1796–1868, commissioner 1829–68).

The nine principles are as follows.

1. The basic mission for which the police exists is to prevent crime and disorder.

2. The ability of the police to perform their duties is dependent upon public approval of police actions.

3. Police must secure the willing co-operation of the public in voluntary observance of the law to be able to secure and maintain the respect of the public.

4. The degree of co-operation of the public that can be secured diminishes proportionately to the necessity of the use of physical force.

5. Police seek and preserve public favour not by pandering to public opinion but by constantly demonstrating absolute impartial service to the law.

6. Police use physical force to the extent necessary to secure observance of the law or to restore order only when the exercise of persuasion, advice and warning is found to be insufficient.

7. Police, at all times, should maintain a relationship with the public that gives reality to the historic tradition that the police are the public and the public are the police; the police being only members of the public who are paid to give full-time attention to duties which are incumbent on every citizen in the interests of community welfare and existence.

8. Police should always direct their actions strictly towards their functions and never appear to usurp the power of the judiciary.

9. The test of the police efficiency is the absence of crime and disorder not the visible evidence of police action in dealing with it.

REFLECTIVE PRACTICE 1.1

LEVEL 4

- Analyse the nine Peelian principles and consider which ones are still applicable to policing today.

- If you were to change any of these principles, which would you change and why?

CRITICAL THINKING ACTIVITY 1.1

LEVEL 4

- Critically analyse the following statement.

Sir Robert Peel is seen as the father of policing and is credited with modernising the police in 1829, but we now know the Glasgow Police Act was 29 years earlier in 1800 and the Act was passed in parliament. So why is Scotland not seen as the birthplace or modern policing?

POLICE OFFICERS

The core duty of the police is to protect the public by detecting and preventing crime. This is established by common law and legislation which gives the police the authority to execute these powers. Police officers are individually responsible for using these powers in accordance with the law; these powers should be necessary and proportionate and compatible with human rights and equalities legislation. Although police officers receive training in the use of these powers, they ultimately have discretion to make their own decisions. They must have a clear rationale for doing so while remaining compliant within the law.

The College of Policing has the responsibility for issuing professional codes of practice (Police Act 1996, s.39A). These codes include a Code of Ethics which complements the policing standards of professional behaviour. These ethics now sit at the heart of the National Decision Making Model, which assists officers to make fair and just decisions.

There are ten standards of professional behaviour (Police Reform Act 2002), which include treating colleagues and members of the public with respect and courtesy, and behaving in a manner that does not discredit the police service or undermine public confidence in it. Any serious breach of these standards may result in the officer becoming the subject of misconduct proceedings, which can result in disciplinary action or dismissal from the police. The misuse of power may also be challenged through civil proceedings or in some cases the criminal courts.

REFLECTIVE PRACTICE 1.2

LEVEL 4

- Consider the following statement.

Peelian principle number five states that police 'seek and preserve public favour not by catering to public opinion but by constantly demonstrating absolute impartial service to the law'. Modern leaders, both police and politicians, struggle with listening to public consensus, and enforcing the law as written without fear or favour.

- In light of the current wave of protests and the introduction of new legislation such as the Police, Crime, Sentencing and Courts Act 2022 in regard to demonstrations, how can law enforcement continue to enforce the law when even routine and appropriate enforcement is called misconduct?

POLICE POWERS

Police powers can be grouped into three categories.

1. **Powers to investigate crime** – including a range of powers to collect evidence needed to identify suspects and support their fair and effective trial.

2. **Powers to prevent crime** – including a range of powers to maintain public order and prevent anti-social behaviour.

3. **Powers to dispose of criminal cases** – allowing police officers to dispose of criminal cases outside of court or charge suspects so they can be prosecuted through the courts.

Each of these is now considered.

INVESTIGATING POWERS

The police have a recognised common law power to carry out their duty to investigate crime. Their power to carry out this duty is now heavily regulated by several important pieces of legislation: the Police and Criminal Evidence Act (PACE) 1984, the Investigatory Powers Act (IPA) 2016 and the Regulation of Investigatory Powers Act (RIPA) 2000.

This section concentrates on police powers available from PACE. The IPA and RIPA are discussed in more detail in another book in this series: *Criminal Investigation* (Stainton and Ewin, 2022).

PACE

This Act was introduced in 1984, following the publication of the Scarman Report in 1981 after the Brixton Riots, and is widely considered to have fundamentally changed the way of policing. The Act regulates police powers in the following areas:

- arrest and detain, question and take biometric details of those suspected of a crime;

- enter private property, search the property and seize evidence;

- stop and search individuals and vehicles.

The Home Office is responsible for publishing and maintaining a set of statutory codes of practice on PACE known as the Codes of Practice. These codes provide guidance to police officers on how to use their powers legally. Section 67 of PACE states that a police officer must adhere to the relevant provisions of the codes while on duty.

There are seven PACE codes covering the following areas:

1. Code A – Stop and search;

2. Code B – Entry, search and seizure;

3. Code C – Detention and custody;

4. Code D – Identifying suspects;

5. Code E and F – Recording of interviews with suspects;

6. Code G – Arrest;

7. Code H – Detention and custody of terrorism suspects.

The Home Secretary must consult police and crime commissioners (PCCs), chief constables, the General Council of the Bar, the Law Society, the Institute of Legal Executives, and any other person they 'think fit' before issuing or revising a PACE code. Twenty major changes to a code must be approved by an affirmative resolution of both Houses of Parliament. This means that both MPs and Lords are required to approve major changes to PACE codes.

The codes are discussed below in the order that they are generally taught in initial police training.

ARREST (CODE G)

Police officers have several main powers of arrest.

- A statutory power (under section 24 of PACE) to arrest, without a warrant, anyone they suspect has committed or is committing a criminal offence when it is necessary.

- Statutory powers to execute arrest warrants issued by the courts.

- Statutory powers to arrest those who fail to answer or breach their bail conditions and those who breach the conditions of a caution.

- There is a limited power to arrest those who breach their anti-social behaviour civil injunction. The power is limited as a warrant is required to make the arrest.

- A common law power to arrest those they suspect have 'breached the peace' or are threatening to do so.

ARREST OF THOSE SUSPECTED OF CRIME

Section 24 of PACE (as amended) provides the police with the statutory power to arrest those they suspect have committed a crime when it is necessary.

An arrest is necessary under section 24 if it is: required to ascertain the name and address of the suspect, protect vulnerable people, prevent injury or damage to property, or support the prompt investigation or prosecution of an offence.

PACE Code G provides police officers with statutory guidance on their section 24 arrest power.

Section 24 of PACE was amended by the Serious Organised Crime and Police Act 2005. The 2005 Act removed a requirement on officers to consider the seriousness of an alleged offence before conducting an arrest without a warrant. Before 2005, officers could only arrest someone without a warrant if they were suspected of committing a serious offence. Now officers can arrest those they suspect of committing any crime without a warrant when it is necessary.

POLICING SPOTLIGHT

SECTION 24 OF PACE 1984 – NECESSITY TEST

- Ascertain the person's name.

- Ascertain the person's address.

- Prevent physical harm to self or another or suffering physical injury.

- Prevent loss of or damage to property.

- Prevent an offence against public decency.

- Prevent an unlawful obstruction of the highway.

⟶

- Protect a child or vulnerable person.

- Prevent any prosecution being hindered by the disappearance of the person in question.

- Allow a prompt and effective investigation of the offence or of the conduct of the person in question.

DETENTION (CODE C)

Part IV and V of PACE provide the police with powers to detain those they have arrested without charge. The detention of a suspect is often crucial to a police investigation. Once detained the police have powers to question the suspect and collect their biometric information. The information collected during detention can help the police determine whether a suspect should be charged with a criminal offence.

The detention of a suspect under PACE is subject to strict time limits. The police should deal with suspects 'expeditiously' and release them 'as soon as the need for detention no longer applies'. Most suspects can only be detained without charge for up to 24 hours. Individuals arrested for serious offences may be detained without charge for up to four days if authorised by senior officers and the courts.

The police should aim to make a charging decision while the suspect is in custody. Suspects who cannot be charged are normally released 'under investigation' but they can be 'bailed' when it is proportionate and necessary to do so. Suspects released on bail are required to report to the police at regular intervals while the investigation is ongoing. The police may attach further conditions to their bail, designed to protect victims and witnesses or preserve evidence. While a suspect is in custody or on bail they can be 'ruled out' of the crime due to further investigations. The police should notify those that have been arrested but are no longer under investigation as soon as practicably possible and release them without delay.

PACE Code C provides statutory guidance on police detention powers. Police forces are required to detain people held under PACE in accordance with the code. The College of Policing has published authorised professional practice (APP) guidance on detention and custody. His Majesty's Inspectorate of Prisons (HMIP) and His Majesty's Inspectorate of Constabulary and Fire & Rescue Services (HMICFRS) have published responsibilities for police custody. They measure police forces against these expectations during their regular inspections of police custody facilities.

STOP AND SEARCH (CODE A)

The police have a variety of statutory powers to 'stop and search' individuals. The power to stop and search is possibly one of the most contentious powers available to the police and is often criticised as it has been proven that the persons stopped are more likely to come from an ethnic minority background than those of a white background. Stop and search powers allow officers to *'allay or confirm suspicions about individuals without exercising their power of arrest'*. There is no common law power to stop and search. Every time the police conduct a stop and search, they must do so on the basis of one of their statutory powers.

There are three types of stop and search powers.

1. Powers which require officers to have 'reasonable grounds' to conduct the search, known as a section 1 PACE search.

2. A power which allows officers to search without reasonable grounds, sometimes known as 'no suspicion' or 'section 60' search after the Criminal Justice and Public Order Act 1994. This power can only be used when authorised by a senior officer based on certain 'pre-conditions'.

3. A power officers can use to search those they 'reasonably suspect' are terrorists. The power for the search is obtained by sections 43 and 44 of the Terrorism Act 2000.

The College of Policing has published authorised professional practice (APP) guidance on stop and search. The Home Office has also published guidance on the best use of stop and search. Stop and search is a particularly controversial police power and remains the subject matter of much debate.

POLICING SPOTLIGHT

TO CONDUCT A SEARCH, YOU MUST GIVE THE SUSPECT CERTAIN INFORMATION, REMEMBERED BY THE MNEMONIC GOWISELY

- **G**rounds for the search.

- **O**bject the officer is searching for.

- **W**arrant, particularly if the officer is in plain clothes.

→

- **I**dentification – proof that the officer is indeed a police officer!

- **S**tation which the officer is attached to.

- **E**ntitlement – any citizen being searched by a police officer is entitled to copies of all paperwork.

- **L**egislation – the legal power which gives the officer the right to stop and search.

- **Y**ou are being detained for the search or for the purpose of... essentially informing the citizen in no uncertain terms about the purpose and nature of the search.

REASONABLE GROUNDS SEARCHES

Most stop and search powers require officers to have 'reasonable grounds' to suspect the person they are searching has prohibited or stolen items. Under section 1 of PACE, officers can stop and search individuals (their person or their vehicle) if they have 'reasonable grounds' to suspect the individual has a bladed/offensive weapon, a stolen item or fireworks. Section 23 of the Misuse of Drugs Act 1971 gives officers a similar power to search those they have 'reasonable grounds' to suspect have controlled drugs on their person.

PRE-CONDITION SEARCHES

Section 60 of the Criminal Justice and Public Order Act 1994 allows uniformed police officers to stop and search anyone who is in a specific area designated by a senior officer, regardless of whether the officer reasonably believes the individual has a prohibited item. However, certain 'pre-conditions' must be met. A pre-condition search can be authorised when senior officers 'reasonably believe' that one of the following conditions has been met.

- Incidents involving serious violence 'may' take place in a locality and that it is 'expedient' to give authorisation on.

- An incident involving serious violence has taken place, the weapon used is in a locality and it is 'expedient' to give authorisation to find it.

- People are carrying dangerous instruments or offensive weapons in a locality.

- Authorisations can initially last for up to 24 hours with superintendents having the power to authorise extensions up to 48 hours.

- While senior officers may authorise a pre-condition search for up to 48 hours at a time, they are required authorise its use for the shortest period necessary.

REFLECTIVE PRACTICE 1.3

LEVEL 4/5

- Analyse the following statement:

Stop and search laws remain very controversial and the possible cause for much racial tension.

- What alternatives to this should the police consider?

ENTRY, SEARCH AND SEIZURE (CODE B)

Part II of PACE provides officers with powers to enter a property, search it and seize evidence. PACE entry and search powers are the most commonly used by the police but there are a total of 176 pieces of legislation which provide relevant authorities with search warrant powers.

PACE Code B provides officers with their statutory guidance. The College of Policing has provided guidance on searching as part of its APP guidance on investigation.

ENTRY

In general, the police need either a search warrant or the consent of the owner to enter private property. However, sections 17 and 18 of PACE allow officers to enter property without a search warrant or consent in specific circumstances.

Under section 17 of PACE, officers can enter a property without a search warrant or consent in order to:

- execute an arrest warrant;

- arrest someone for a serious offence;

- recapture someone who has escaped from custody;

- save 'life or limb' or prevent serious damage to property;

- prevent a breach of the peace.

Section 18 of PACE allows officers to enter and search the property of someone that is under arrest for a serious offence with the authorisation of an inspector.

SEARCH

Under section 8 of PACE, officers can apply to the courts for search warrants when they have reasonable grounds for believing that they are likely to find materials that would be of substantial value to the investigation of a serious offence.

SEIZURE

Generally, if the police are searching for a person or premises with a warrant, under a specific statutory power or with the consent of the occupier, they can seize anything they reasonably suspect has evidential value or has been obtained through crime.

Sections 19–22 of PACE give officers general powers of seizure. Part II of the Criminal Justice and Police Act 2001 allows officers to seize evidence so it can be examined elsewhere. The Proceeds of Crime Act 2002 (POCA) provides officers with the power to seize cash to the value of £1000 and above if they think it was obtained by, or is to be used in, crime.

Other than cash seized under POCA, seized property (provided it is not prohibited by law such as drugs or firearms) is released by the police once they are satisfied that it is no longer needed for the purposes of their investigation.

Cash seized under POCA can be detained (temporarily seized) and forfeited (permanently confiscated) irrespective of the outcome or progress of a criminal investigation. The police must apply for a court order to detain cash beyond 48 hours. They can also apply for the court to issue an order forfeiting the cash. As this is a civil process, the courts must only be satisfied that on the balance of probabilities the cash was obtained via (or meant for use in) crime in order to authorise its detention or forfeiture.

PREVENTION POWERS

The police's power to prevent crime is largely derived from their common law duty to protect the public and maintain the 'King's peace'. This rather outdated term derives from the Latin *pax regis*, meaning the common law concept of the maintenance of public order. The police also have some legislative powers to prevent disorder associated with protests, certain types of trespass and anti-social behaviour.

BREACH OF THE PEACE

The police have common law powers to maintain the 'King's peace'. These powers allow them to take action to stop or prevent a 'breach of the peace'. For example, officers may make an arrest or enforce a cordon.

While there is no formal definition of 'breach of the peace', it is generally accepted to occur when someone or their property is harmed or likely to be harmed, or a person is in fear of being harmed through an assault, an affray, a riot or other disturbances.

The threat of 'breach of the peace' must be immediate to justify an arrest to prevent it. 'Breaching the peace' is not a criminal offence. Those arrested for breach of the peace cannot be charged but they may still be held on remand. Under Section 115 of the Magistrates' Courts Act 1980, magistrates have 'binding over' powers to hold people in remand to keep the common peace.

Under subsection 89(2) of the Police Act 1996 it is an offence to resist or wilfully obstruct a constable in the execution of their duty. Therefore, officers may arrest those who fail to comply with an instruction made in order to prevent a breach of the peace. Those found guilty of this offence can be imprisoned for up to three months.

USE OF FORCE

Police officers can use proportionate and necessary force in the course of their duties. Their common law powers provide them with authority to use force. Section 3 of the Criminal Law Act 1967 authorises the use of reasonable force to prevent crime or assist a lawful arrest. Section 117 of PACE authorises police officers to use reasonable force to exercise their PACE powers. The College of Policing has provided guidance on the use of force in their APP guidance on public order. They must use the *'minimum amount of force necessary to achieve the required result'* and they must be able to account for their use of force utilising the National Decision Making Model previously discussed.

There are ten key principles governing the use of force by the police service. These principles were written by HMICFRS and have been endorsed by the College of Policing.

1. Police officers have a general duty to protect the public, prevent crime and investigate crime.

2. Police officers may use force to exercise this duty. They may also use force in self-defence or in the defence of others.

3. Police officers shall, as far as possible, apply non-violent methods before resorting to any use of force.

4. When force is used it should be exercised with restraint. It should be the minimum amount honestly and reasonably judged to be necessary.

5. Lethal or potentially lethal force should only be used in self-defence or in the defence of others against the threat of death or serious injury.

6. Police officers should consider the implications of using force against children or vulnerable people.

7. Police operations should be planned to minimise the use of force.

8. Individual officers are accountable and responsible for their use of force and must be able to justify their actions in law.

9. The use of force should be reported and recorded as soon as possible.

10. Senior officers should consider the safety of their personnel when deploying them in a context where force may be used.

PROTESTS

Part II of the Public Order Act 1986 provides the police with powers to manage protests causing or likely to cause disorder. This Act provides the police with three powers.

1. It requires that individuals notify the police when they are planning a protest march.

2. It allows the police to request a protest march is prohibited if they have a serious public order concern. The police have more limited powers to request that certain types of static protests are prohibited.

3. It allows the police to impose conditions on any protests they suspect will cause serious damage to property, serious disruption or will incite unlawful behaviour.

ANTI-SOCIAL BEHAVIOUR

The Anti-social Behaviour, Crime and Policing Act 2014 provides several public sector bodies with powers to prevent and tackle anti-social behaviour. This Act repealed and replaced previous legislation and was designed to consolidate the powers available to tackle anti-social behaviour.

There are now six specific powers, four of which apply to the police, designed to tackle anti-social behaviour. The Home Office maintains statutory guidance for frontline professionals on the powers in the 2014 Act.

The four powers available to the police are as follows.

1. **Dispersal powers** – police officers can direct people they suspect are behaving anti-socially to leave a specific area. The use of this power must be authorised by an officer of least the rank of inspector.

2. **Closure powers** – police inspectors can issue an order temporarily restricting access to premises associated with anti-social behaviour. Superintendents can extend the restrictions for a limited period or ask the courts to restrict access for longer if it is necessary. Local authorities also have closure powers.

3. **ASB injunctions** – police forces (and several other public sector bodies) can apply to the courts for an injunction to be issued against any person (aged ten or older) who has committed persistent anti-social behaviour. Injunctions can prevent individuals from engaging in certain behaviour and/or require them to attend classes or sessions, for example attending a support group for addiction.

4. **Community protection notices (CPNs)** – police officers can issue a CPN to an adult (aged 16 or over), business or organisation whose persistent anti-social behaviour is having a 'detrimental effect... on the quality of life of those in the locality'. A CPN can require an individual, business or organisation to stop doing specified things, do specified things or take reasonable steps to achieve a specified result. For example, a CPN may be issued to an individual who has rubbish in their garden, requiring them to clear it. Local authorities and some social landlords also have the power to issue CPNs.

Local councils must also consult their local police force when considering whether to issue a public spaces protection order (PSPOs). PSPOs allow councils to designate activities as prohibited in specific areas.

DISPOSAL POWERS

The police have powers to 'dispose' of cases they handle. The police can dispose of a case in two ways: they can either charge an individual with a criminal offence, or they can issue an 'out-of-court' disposal. The police are not able to dispose of every case they handle; some investigations go cold when they cannot obtain enough evidence and some cases do not get investigated. The police may decide not to investigate a case if there is a lack of evidence that a crime took place, insufficient lines of inquiry to pursue or simply because they decide to focus their resources on higher-priority cases.

CHARGING

The police have powers to charge those where there is 'sufficient evidence' to show that they have committed an offence they were arrested for. The Crown Prosecution Service (CPS) is responsible for prosecuting cases charged by the police in the courts. The police must adhere to the Director of Public Prosecution's (DPP, the head of the CPS) guidance on charging when making charging decisions This is statutory guidance issued under section 37A of the Police and Criminal Evidence Act 1984.

The police may consult the CPS at any point during their investigation of a crime, but they can (and do) make some charging decisions without CPS advice. There are certain cases where they must consult prosecutors. In these cases, the decision to charge is ultimately taken by the CPS. The police must consult the CPS before charging indictable-only offences (offences which must be tried at a Crown Court). These are the most serious crimes. Indictable-only offences include the following.

- Either-way offences (offences that could be tried at either a magistrates' or Crown Court) other than shoplifting that are either likely to be tried at a Crown Court or where a 'not guilty' plea is anticipated.

- Violent disorder, affray, causing grievous bodily harm, wounding or actual bodily harm, a sex offence where the victim is a child, and any offence under the Licensing Act 2003.

- Any case classified as a hate crime or domestic violence.

- Any case involving a death.

- Any case connected with terrorism or official secrets.

- Any case which requires the consent of the Director of Public Prosecutions or the Attorney General to prosecute.

CHARGING TESTS

There are two tests which guide all charging decisions: the Full Code Test and the Threshold Test. The CPS reviews police charging decisions against these tests. Cases that do not meet the tests will not be prosecuted and may be handed back to the police for further investigation or to be disposed of 'out of court'.

FULL CODE TEST

Most cases will not proceed to charge until the Full Code Test is met. This test has two stages: the evidential stage and the public interest stage.

Those considering a charge must first be satisfied that there is enough evidence to suggest that the suspect is likely to be convicted at trial. The courts must be satisfied 'beyond reasonable doubt' that the accused committed the offence to convict.

When there is enough evidence, those deliberating a charge must next consider if it is in the public interest for the suspect to be charged. There are several factors which help determine this: the severity of the crime, the suspect's culpability, the harm caused to the victim and the impact on the community. The police may choose to dispose of cases 'out of court' that are not in the public interest to charge.

THRESHOLD TEST

Cases which fail the evidential stage of the Full Code Test may proceed to charge if they pass the Threshold Test. Only a limited number of cases will qualify for charge via the Threshold Test. There are five conditions that must be met for a case to pass.

1. The 'reasonable grounds' condition – there must be reasonable grounds to suspect that the individual committed the offence.

2. The 'further evidence' condition – decision makers must be satisfied that further evidence can be obtained to provide a realistic prospect of conviction.

3. The 'seriousness' condition – the alleged offence must be so serious as to justify an immediate charging decision.

4. The 'bail' condition – the suspect must not qualify for bail.

5. The 'public interest' condition – it must be in the public interest for the suspect to be charged.

POLICING SPOTLIGHT

PC Jones is out on night foot patrol in the city centre. At his briefing session he has been informed by his sergeant that there has been a high number of night-time burglaries in the city centre. PC Jones sees Sam Smith, a local boy who is known to him from previous dealings with him and other members of the family. PC Jones approaches Smith and asks him where he has been and where he is going. Smith does not reply.

PC Jones starts to search Smith, who objects by pushing PC Jones away. PC Jones automatically arrests Smith but does not caution him or tell him why he is being arrested.

Smith is taken to the local police station. Before entering the custody suite, PC Jones searches Smith and finds ten packs of cigarettes inside his jacket.

Upon entering the custody suite, PC Jones informs the custody sergeant that he had arrested Smith on suspicion of theft. Smith's detention is authorised and he is placed in a cell.

PC Jones, in an effort to impress, goes with a colleague to Smith's home address. This has not been authorised. The door is opened by Smith's father, who refuses to let PC Jones or his colleague in. Both officers enter the house using force and conduct a search. During the search, several unpacked computers are recovered. PC Jones arrests Mr Smith for obstructing a police officer.

REFLECTIVE PRACTICE 1.4

LEVEL 4/5

Consider and comment on the actions of PC Jones in relation to the following:

- the legality of the initial stop and search;

- the legality of the arrest;

- the legality of the second search;

- the legality of the search of Smith's home and the property recovered;

- the arrest of Mr Smith.

EVIDENCE-BASED POLICING

INTRODUCTION

Evidence-based policing is utilised by police officers and staff to review
the available evidence and inform and challenge policies, practices and decisions. This
can be supported by collaboration with academics and partners utilising appropriate
research methods and sources for the question being asked.

AN EXAMPLE

Previously, an inspector had decided to hand out leaflets to revellers to discourage them
from engaging in disorder on leaving public houses. Over 200 leaflets were handed out –
the result was that there was a 30 per cent drop in the cases of disorder. The inspector
proposes that a similar action should take place force-wide.

Evidence-based policing links critical thinking and research together to understand the
true effect of the leaflet drop.

OUTCOME OF FURTHER RESEARCH

On the night, it was raining heavily, and local public houses reported a drop in attendance
of 40 per cent.

The figures used for comparison were taken from the week previously when it had been
fine weather and an important football match had taken place on the same day. There
were also fewer resources available on the night in question.

CONCLUSION

On face value, the original report shows a reduction in public disorder; however, once
further facts are researched and critical thinking is applied it demonstrates that the
exercise was not as successful as first thought.

SUMMARY OF KEY CONCEPTS

This chapter has discussed the formation of the police service and the powers available to the police. The following key concepts were covered.

- Sir Robert Peel is credited with the introduction of the Peelian principles.

- The Peelian principles are applicable to modern-day policing.

- Police powers are formed by a combination of common law powers and legislation.

- The Police and Criminal Evidence Act 1984 is divided into various codes and it important to have a working knowledge of them.

- Police powers and policing interact with each other.

CHECK YOUR KNOWLEDGE

1. Who is credited with the creation of nine principles of policing?

2. What year was the Metropolitan Police Act legislated?

3. The Scarman Report is credited with the creation of what?

4. What code within PACE allows an officer to conduct a stop and search?

5. How many pieces of legislation cover the searching of private property?

Sample answers are provided at the end of this book.

FURTHER READING

BOOKS

Bryant, R and Bryant, S (2021) *Blackstone's Handbook for Policing Students*.
Oxford: Oxford University Press.
Chapter 1 of this book discusses police powers and an officer's duties.

Dicey, A V (1886) *Introduction to the Study of the Law of the Constitution*. Indianapolis,
IN: Liberty Fund.
This title discusses the rule of law and gives the reader an in-depth understanding of the
subject.

Newman, T (2005) *Handbook of Policing*. Abingdon: Willan Publishing.
This book concentrates on the role of a police officer and covers the duties of a police
officer.

WEBSITES

College of Policing (2022) APP (Authorised Professional Practice). [online] Available
at: www.app.college.police.uk (accessed 6 October 2022).
The College of Policing APP web pages provide a searchable resource, covering many
aspects of police powers.

Police and Criminal Evidence Act 1984 [online] Available at: www.legislation.gov.uk/
ukpga/1984/60/contents (accessed 6 October 2022).
This site provides further reading on the Police and Criminal Evidence Act 1984.

CHAPTER 2
STOP AND SEARCH

LEARNING OBJECTIVES

AFTER READING THIS CHAPTER YOU WILL BE ABLE TO:

⚙ clearly describe police stop and search powers;

⚙ understand the information required to conduct a search;

⚙ understand how police powers and policing interact with each other;

⚙ explain the use of various police powers.

INTRODUCTION

This chapter discusses the powers given to officers to stop and search individuals on the street if they have reasonable grounds to believe that someone has on their person or with them items to indicate that they have been involved in a criminal activity, are about to be involved in criminality or are in possession of a prohibited article. These powers are available within the Police and Criminal Evidence Act (PACE) 1984.

Prior to the introduction of the Act, police officers relied upon 'sus' law to conduct stop and searches where officers were only required to state that they were suspicious of the person they had stopped to search. It is argued that the use of such powers led to the Brixton Riots in 1981 where Operation Swamp was utilised to stop and search black males in relation to a recent rise in crime. Lord Scarman's inquiry into the riots acknowledged that stop and search was necessary to combat crime but held concerns over the use of 'sus' laws. Lord Scarman called for the replacement of 'sus' laws with national, safeguarded stop and search legislation. He also called for community consultation and statutory liaison communities.

In 1984, the Police and Criminal Evidence Act (PACE) was introduced and included section 1, which gave officers the power to stop and search individuals if they had responsible grounds to believe the person is involved in crime or is about to commit crime or has prohibited items with them.

There are currently 19 different powers available to police officers to stop and search an individual for various reasons, the most common of those are section 1 of PACE and section 23 of the Misuse of Drugs Act 1971.

Stop and search powers still attract controversy (Vomfell and Stewart, 2021) and following the 1993 murder of Stephen Lawrence, in 1999 Lord Macpherson revealed the disproportionate use of stop and search among members of black and Asian communities, which led to accusations of police discrimination and heightened distrust of the police within these communities and called for all stops, whether a search was then conducted or not, to be recorded.

While this chapter will discuss the powers and responsibilities afforded by section 1 of the Police and Criminal Evidence Act 1984, other stop and search powers are available such as:

- Misuse of Drugs Act 1971;

- Criminal Justice and Public Order Act 1994;

- Terrorism Act 2000;

- Proceeds of Crime Act 2002;

- Animal Welfare Act 2006;

- Psychoactive Substances Act 2016.

The following activities will assist you in developing your knowledge.

REFLECTIVE PRACTICE 2.1

LEVEL 4

- Consider the brief history of stop and search within England and Wales.

- Stop and search is regarded as an effective tool to tackle crime; however, what effects does this have on our community relations when innocent people are being stopped?

CRITICAL THINKING ACTIVITY 2.1

LEVEL 4

- Critically analyse the following statement.

Stop and search within England and Wales remains a controversial topic with evidence that more black members of society are stopped and searched than their white counterparts.

- Why is this the case and what can be done to address this issue?

WHAT ARE REASONABLE GROUNDS?

Code A of the Police and Criminal Evidence Act 1984 states that '*Stop and search powers must be used fairly... and without unlawful discrimination. Police officers must have due regard to the need to eliminate unlawful discrimination, harassment and victimization.*'

In order to ensure that the public continue to be satisfied with police stop and searches, it is imperative that all searches are conduced fairly and that the individual does not feel targeted by the officers conducting the searches. Therefore, it is never appropriate to stop and search a person based on protected characteristics, outlined below.

According to section 149 of the Equality Act 2010, when officers use stop and search powers they must have due regard of the need to eliminate discrimination, harassment, victimisation and any other conduct that is prohibited by or under the Act. Officers should:

- advance equality of opportunity between persons who share a relevant protected characteristic and persons who do not share it;

- foster good relations between persons who share a relevant protected characteristic and persons who do not share it.

Therefore, any search based on any of the following characteristics would be unlawful: age, disability, gender reassignment, marriage and civil partnership, pregnancy and maternity, race, religion or belief, sex and sexual orientation.

Searches must be based on objective factors: '*Search is more likely to be effective, legitimate and secure public confidence if reasonable grounds for suspicion are based on a range of objective factors*' (PACE Code A). To ensure that all persons are treated fairly, an objective test must be utilised to exercise stop and search powers and the officer must have reasonable grounds for suspicion.

- First, the officer must have formed a *genuine suspicion* in their own mind that they will find the object for which the search power being exercised allows them to search.

- Second, the suspicion that the object will be found must be *reasonable*. This means that there must be an *objective* basis for that suspicion based on facts, information and/or intelligence which are relevant to the likelihood that the object in question will be found.

This is an objective test in that it expects that a reasonable person given the same information would also suspect that the individual is carrying the item.

Reasonable grounds for suspicion can never be supported by personal factors, such as previous convictions and assumptions that certain groups are involved in criminality. Paragraph 2.2B of PACE Code A states that personal factors cannot be used as the reason for a stop and search alone or in combination with each other, meaning that you cannot combine personal factors to achieve reasonable suspicion, ie previous convictions and race/ethnicity.

Therefore, an officer cannot decide to stop and search a person based on:

- their physical appearance;

- they have been in trouble before;

- the officer's knowledge of whether or not they have previous convictions;

- the assumption that because a person, for example, lives on a particular street, adopts a specific lifestyle or is a young person wearing a hoodie, they are likely to be carrying a prohibited item.

This does not mean that officers cannot stop and search individuals based on personal factors but they must be supported by other factors, such as intelligence or that the individual matches a description given.

REASONABLE GROUNDS FOR SUSPICION BASED ON INFORMATION OR INTELLIGENCE

Reasonable grounds for suspicion can be developed utilising information and intelligence that has been obtained from members of the public or other channels such as fellow officers. Officers who are conducting stop and searches utilising information and intelligence are more likely to have successful stop and searches (Stanier, 2016). All information and intelligence should be accurate, current and relate to articles being carried by a person or in a vehicle in the locality. Access to accurate intelligence and information about local crime patterns is paramount to serving officers to ensure they can build reasonable grounds to stop and search individuals. However, officers should be prepared to probe the intelligence available to ensure that it is still relevant.

Officers can build their reasonable grounds for a search based on the behaviour of a person in combination with the circumstances, for example a person seen in the middle of the night in dark clothing carrying a bag in the vicinity of a recent burglary. The officer must be able to provide a clear, full and detailed explanation of the behaviours that made them generally suspect the person. The following reflective practice discusses this.

REFLECTIVE PRACTICE 2.2

LEVEL 4/5

- Analyse the following statement:

PC Jones sees a male running away from a shop front that has been smashed and merchandise is on the floor. They give chase, catching the male and conduct a stop and search.

- Consider what factors PC Jones has utilised to conduct the stop and search.

LEGAL REQUIREMENTS

Officers must act and be seen to act in accordance with the law to ensure that the legitimacy of the police is maintained, and that the public continue to have faith in the police. Acting in this manner will give officers protection and if something does go wrong, they will be able to demonstrate they conducted the stop and search within correct procedures. Should you fail to act within the law, any 'finds' may be subject to challenge within a court of law.

As the police are state agents there is an obligation to act in accordance with the law when exercising their powers that may interfere with an individual's rights. Officers are therefore required to ensure they act within the boundaries of the European Convention on Human Rights (ECHR) and the Human Rights Act 1998, which incorporated the ECHR into UK law. Stop and search has the potential to breach an individual's rights under Article 5 (liberty and security) and Article 8 (respect for private and family life). Failure to comply with correct stop and search practices could lead to breaches of the Human Rights Act.

An officer must not search a person if there is no specific power to do so even if they consent to being searched (PACE Code A); the only exception would be if search for entry to a premises is a condition of entry.

For a stop and search to be legal it must have legal basis and be lawfully applied, by using powers provided by legislation for the particular circumstances, including ensuring the extent of the search is necessary and proportionate.

EVIDENCE-BASED POLICING

STOP AND SEARCH DEVELOPMENT

Stop and search powers remain a controversial topic within policing with the Home Secretary arguing in 2022 that there is a need for officers to conduct more stop and searches and additionally lifting all restrictions on section 60 stop and search powers (*Guardian*, 2022). However, with the introduction of formal stop and search powers in 1984 in the Police and Criminal Evidence Act (PACE), there has been a need to monitor the effectiveness of such powers on the community. Both the Scarman Report (Scarman, 1986) and the Macpherson Report (Macpherson, 1999) called for a more structured and balanced approach to stop and search, which originally led to the introduction of PACE 1984. However, it can be argued that, using an evidence-based practice, there is a need to constantly research the impact of such powers on the communities the police serve. One question for the reader to consider, incorporating evidence-based practice, is where is the evidence that removing the restrictions on section 60 searches will increase the number of offenders brought to court and what will the effects on the community be?

POLICING SPOTLIGHT

It is 5pm on a Monday afternoon. PC Abbott sees a male they recognise as a local thief, who has been arrested a number of times previously. His name is Adam King and he is 24 years old. PC Abbott walks over to the male and tells him he is being detained for a search and no more. PC Abbott searches Adam and finds nothing and tells him to clear off. No paperwork is completed.

REFLECTIVE PRACTICE 2.3

Consider the actions of PC Abbott, and evaluate whether:

- they have acted unlawfully;

- the grounds of the search were acceptable.

THE DECISION TO SEARCH

As previously discussed, any decision to search must be objectively proportionate to the circumstances. Where an officer has sufficient grounds to search, the search is likely to be proportionate, and consideration should then be given to the extent of the search. PACE Code A states that 'the decision must be judged on a case-by-case basis according to the circumstances applicable at the time of the proposed searches'. Regard must be had to:

- the number of items suspected of being carried;

- the nature of those items and the risk they pose;

- the number of individuals to be searched.

An example of this is the case of Howarth v Commissioner of Police of the Metropolis [2011] EWHC 2818 (Admin), which was concerned with the searches of a number of demonstrators on a train suspected of carrying objects to cause criminal damage. The court was asked to consider the following points with regard to whether the searches went beyond the reasonable responses of a police officer to the intelligence received.

Key considerations included the following:

- intelligence and past experience gave a reasonable anticipation of significant damage;

- the group, while not small, was confined to a number of passengers on a train;

- steps were taken to identify those searched as protestors;

- the searches were of the type commonly used in public places and on entrance to entertainment and travel venues;

- the organisers of the demonstration had not liaised with the police in advance, which justified enhanced concern.

The court concluded, based on these factors, that the searches were not excessive in character when taking into account the nature of the suspicion held.

DETENTION FOR THE PURPOSE OF SEARCH

All persons subject to a stop and search must be advised that they are being detained for the purpose of a search, and they may also be advised that under section 117 of PACE, reasonable force may be used to conduct the search. If the person has not been advised that they have been detained, then section 117 is not activated. Police officers should be mindful that the act of searching someone is counted as reasonable force. Even though the power to use reasonable force is available, those conducting searches should always seek to complete the task with co-operation. Any use of reasonable force as set out in section 3 of the Criminal Law Act 1967 should only be used in the prevention of crime, or in effecting or assisting in the lawful arrest of offenders or suspected offenders or of persons unlawfully at large.

Persons being searched should not be routinely handcuffed; each case should be judged on its merits and be proportionate to the situation.

HOW TO CONDUCT THE SEARCH

All searches should be completed as soon as possible and carried out with courtesy, consideration and respect for the person concerned. The person should be detained no longer than is necessary to complete the search and conducted within a reasonable travelling distance of where the person was stopped. The effectiveness of the search and thoroughness must not be excessive; the search must be based on the reasonable grounds that are being utilised for the search. For example, if the person is suspected of having a large item then searching pockets would not be acceptable. On the other hand, if the item is small then the search can be more detailed and might include pockets. The search of children and vulnerable people is another key consideration. PACE Code A recognises the limitations and expectations of the Children Act 2004, section 11, and the need to safeguard and promote the welfare of all persons under the age of 18. Although Code A does not specify where searches of children or vulnerable adults should be completed, officers should consider the need for an appropriate adult to be present and for them to attend as soon as possible. The search could take place at a home address or police station as long as it is proportionate.

REMOVING CLOTHING

When searching a person in public, the police officer can only require the person to remove the following clothing: jacket, outer coat and gloves (JOG). Any item that is believed to be used to deliberately conceal their identity can be removed under section 60AA of the Criminal Justice and Public Order Act 1994. If the person refuses to comply, the police officer cannot forcibly remove the item; however, the person is committing an imprisonable offence and can be arrested.

Considering the notion of reasonable grounds for the search, an officer may, as part of a JOG search:

- place their hand in the inside pocket of outer clothing;

- feel around the inside of collars, socks and shoes;

- search hair as long as there are no restrictions on the removal of headgear, for example, for religious reasons.

If the search requires the removal of religious headgear this should be conducted out of public view and, if practicable, such removal should be completed out of sight of the opposite sex of the person being searched.

SEARCHING OUT OF PUBLIC VIEW

A more thorough search may be conducted out of public view. This might involve the removal of more than JOG, but not exposing intimate parts, and may be conducted either in a police van or a police station. Such a search must be conducted by an officer of the same sex and not in the presence of a member of the opposite sex unless specifically requested by the person.

SEARCH INVOLVING EXPOSURE OF INTIMATE PARTS

Any search exposing the intimate parts of the body (also referred to as a 'strip search') is the most intrusive form of search permitted. See Code H, Annex A – 10 of PACE 1984.

It should not be a routine extension of any search and should only be used where is it necessary and reasonable considering the object of the search.

While no additional authority is required to conduct such a search, it is best practice to obtain direction from a supervisor to ensure that the search is proportionate and legal. Any such searches should be conducted within a police station with persons of the same sex. The search must be conducted where the person being searched cannot be seen by any other person than those completing the search. A minimum of two officers are required to conduct the search, and in the case of a minor, an appropriate adult should be one of the persons. An appropriate adult in the first instance would be a parent or a person who has guardianship of the child. Proper regard should be given to the sensitivity and vulnerability of the person and every reasonable effort made to secure the person's co-operation and minimise embarrassment. They should not normally be required to remove all their clothes at the same time. For example, a person should be allowed to remove clothing above the waist and redress before being required to remove further clothing, subject to necessity in the circumstances. If necessary to assist the search, the person may be asked to facilitate a visual examination of the genital and anal area but no physical contact may be made with any bodily orifice. The strip search should be conducted as quickly as possible and the person allowed to dress as soon as it is completed.

If, as a result of a search exposing intimate parts of the body, an item the officer is searching for can be seen in a body orifice other than the mouth, it cannot be seized as that would constitute an intimate search. Intimate searches are not permitted under any circumstance under stop and search powers.

REFLECTIVE PRACTICE 2.4

LEVEL 4

When conducting stop and searches, police officers have a power to remove the following:

- jacket;

→

- **o**uter coat;

- **g**loves.

Considering the following scenario, which items can PC Crawfish ask the person to remove?

PC Crawfish is conducting a search of a female offender; it is the middle of winter and it is very cold. The suspect is wearing among other things a jacket, gloves, a scarf and ear warmers; they also have another large coat on as well.

COMMUNICATION

While there is a need to complete stop and search procedures, officers need to be aware that there is a continued need to build the trust of the community; dissatisfaction with stop and searches has shown that people are less likely to trust the police. Members of the public are less likely to be dissatisfied with stop and search when:

- they do not feel unfairly targeted;

- officers give them a good and credible reason for the encounter;

- they are treated politely and with respect by officers;

- the encounter does not last a long time.

When officers conduct stop and search procedures in line with legislation and best practice while demonstrating fair decision making and respectful treatment of those stopped, this will assist in continuing to demonstrate that stop and search powers are legitimate. To assist with this, section 38 of the Police Reform Act 2002 states that during stop and search encounters officers must comply with the professional standards of conduct, especially the code of ethics; communicate effectively with people; and treat people with dignity and respect. This means applying the Peelian principles and standards of professional behaviour (Lumsdon, 2017).

Communication with a stopped person should be clear and concise, and full reasons for the search should be given. To maximise the person's understanding before starting the search, officers exercising stop and search powers must adopt the following steps in accordance with the **GOWISELY** acronym.

- **G**rounds of search.

- **O**bject of search.

- **W**arrant card.

- **I**dentity of officer, the officer's name and number.

- **S**tation attached to.

- **E**ntitlement to a copy of the search record (ie within three months).

- **L**egal power used.

- **Y**ou are detained for the purposes of a search (tell them this).

HOW TO RECORD THE STOP AND SEARCH

Stop and searches should be recorded in line with force procedure. Police forces record the ethnicity of the person being stopped to improve monitoring and disproportionality and, most importantly, to ensure that stop and search is being used in a fair and effective manner. It is mandatory that every stop and search is recorded.

The record must always include the minimum details as specified in Code A:

- a note of the self-defined ethnicity of the person being searched (if provided) and, if different, their ethnicity as perceived by the officer conducting the search;

- the date, time and place the person was searched;

- the object of the search, ie the article the officer was searching for, such as offensive weapon or bladed article, drugs, stolen property or items for use in theft or criminal damage;

- a clear explanation of the legal basis for the search, ie the reasonable grounds for suspicion or authorisation;

- the identity of all officers conducting the search – where recording the names would cause a risk to the officer or if the investigation relates to terrorism, a warrant/identification number and duty station can be given instead.

USING BODY-WORN VIDEO TO RECORD INFORMATION

Where available, body-worn video should be used in accordance with force policy. The standard approach is that body-worn video should be activated so as to capture all relevant information in the time leading up to the person being detained for a search, the conduct of the search itself and the subsequent conclusion of the encounter.

Where a strip search takes place, officers should record the encounter in accordance with force policy, but should cover the camera (or direct it away from the person) whenever intimate body parts are exposed. Audio recording should remain activated. The officer should explain to the person that the recording is for the protection of all parties and reassure them that intimate parts will not be filmed.

Retention periods for body-worn video footage are a matter of force policy due to variation in capabilities and cost implications. When developing their retention policy, forces should bear in mind that search records can be requested for up to three months under paragraph 3.8(e) of Code A.

SUMMARY OF KEY CONCEPTS

This chapter has discussed stop and search and the powers afforded to police officers by section 1 of the Police and Criminal Evidence Act 1984. The following key concepts were covered.

⚙ **Officers must have reasonable grounds to conduct a search.**

⚙ **Stop and search is an important tool within policing but must be completed proportionately.**

⬣ Code A of the Police and Criminal Evidence Act 1984 covers stop and search powers.

⬣ Police powers and policing interact with each other.

CHECK YOUR KNOWLEDGE

1. What year did Lord Scarman complete his inquiry?

2. When was 'sus' law repealed?

3. The Police and Criminal Evidence Act was enacted in which year?

4. Which acronym helps you remember the process of a stop and search?

5. How many pieces of legislation cover stop and search powers?

Sample answers are provided at the end of this book.

FURTHER READING

BOOKS

Bryant, R and Bryant, S (2021) *Blackstone's Handbook for Policing Students.* Oxford: Oxford University Press.
Chapter 1 of this book discusses police powers and an officer's duties.

Newman, T (2005) *Handbook of Policing.* Abingdon: Willan Publishing
The author of this book concentrates on the role of a police officer and covers the duties of a police officer.

WEBSITES

College of Policing (2022) APP (Authorised Professional Practice). [online] Available at: www.app.college.police.uk (accessed 6 October 2022).
The College of Policing APP web pages provide a searchable resource, covering guidance on many aspects of police powers.

Police and Criminal Evidence Act 1984 [online] Available at: www.legislation.gov.uk/ukpga/1984/60/contents (accessed 6 October 2022).
This site provides further reading on the Police and Criminal Evidence Act 1984.

CHAPTER 3
ARREST AND CUSTODY PROCEDURES

LEARNING OBJECTIVES

AFTER READING THIS CHAPTER YOU WILL BE ABLE TO:

- describe arrest procedures and the power of arrest;

- detail the information required to conduct an arrest;

- understand custody procedures and your requirements as an arresting officer;

- explain the use of various police powers.

INTRODUCTION

The power to arrest a person on suspicion of committing a criminal act is one of the greatest powers afforded to a police officer as it effectively enables a warranted officer to remove a person's liberty. The power to arrest an individual is given to an officer via the Police and Criminal Evidence Act (PACE) 1984 Code G.

It is therefore imperative that police officers understand the law and the procedures for detaining someone, carrying out an arrest and taking that person into custody. It is crucial that when removing someone's liberty, a professional approach is taken and you must be clear about the powers that you are using. When utilising these powers, they must be shown to be justified and proportionate in line with the Human Rights Act 1998 and the provisions of PACE 1984.

After discussing the powers of arrest, the chapter goes on to discuss the detention of persons and why it is necessary to conduct relevant risk assessments of all persons detained to ensure that the detained person is well cared for as per PACE and the safer detention and handling of persons in police custody guidance (ACPO, 2012). The following activities explore this area.

REFLECTIVE PRACTICE 3.1

LEVEL 4

- Consider the effects on a person when they are arrested for the first time; what are their expectations?

- To remove a person's liberty is regarded as the greatest power bestowed on a police officer. Do you agree with this statement and why?

CRITICAL THINKING ACTIVITY 3.1

LEVEL 4

- Critically analyse the following statement.

The police power to arrest on suspicion that a person has committed a criminal offence and suspicion that the person is guilty of committing the suspected offence is a too far-reaching power and should be restricted.

POWERS OF ARREST

All police officers are members of the community they serve but are given the extra responsibility of having the power to arrest someone. The power of arrest is afforded to you by acts of parliament in various elements of legislation; it is important that you understand what your powers are and where they come from.

POLICE AND CRIMINAL EVIDENCE ACT (PACE) 1984

PACE Code G states that the power of arrest is applicable to anyone:

- who is about to commit an offence or is in the act of committing an offence;

- whom the officer has reasonable grounds for suspecting is about to commit an offence or to be committing an offence;

- whom the officer has reasonable grounds to suspect of being guilty of an offence which he or she has reasonable grounds for suspecting has been committed;

- who is guilty of an offence which has been committed or anyone whom the officer has reasonable grounds for suspecting to be guilty of that offence.

There are additional powers of arrest shown in PACE Code G, 1A. Make sure you are aware of these powers as they will be useful for your operational roles.

EVIDENCE-BASED POLICING

THE NEED FOR ARREST AND CUSTODY

The utilisation of evidence-based practice within policing allows the police to consider the implication of arrest and custody and ultimately the workings of the criminal justice system. It is evident that the procedures of this practice have led to the

→

development of out-of-court disposals to deliver justice in a timely fashion to the victim of the crime. By continuing to evaluate the process of the need to arrest and detain persons, it allows researchers to discover the benefits of the introduction of these systems. Chapter 4 discusses the use of out-of-court disposals and the continued evidence-based practice in regard to the effectiveness of such practices, therefore demonstrating that such practices are not limited to one subject area but can be used to look at all aspects of policing and develop new ways of practice.

THE ARREST OF THOSE SUSPECTED OF A CRIME

Section 24 of PACE (as amended) provides the police with the statutory power to arrest those they suspect have committed a crime when they *believe* it is **necessary**.

An arrest is **necessary** under section 24 so long as:

- it is required to ascertain the name and address of the suspect;

- a person's address cannot be readily ascertained if they fail or refuse to give it when asked;

- it is to prevent the person from:

  - causing physical injury to themselves or any other person;

  - suffering physical injury;

  - causing loss or damage to property;

  - committing an offence against public decency (only applies where members of the public going about their normal business cannot reasonably be expected to avoid the person in question);

  - causing an unlawful obstruction of the highway.

- it protects a child or other vulnerable person;

- it allows for a prompt and effective investigation.

PACE Code G also provides police officers with statutory guidance on their section 24 arrest power.

Section 24 of PACE was amended by the Serious Organised Crime and Police Act 2005. The 2005 Act removed a requirement on officers to consider the seriousness of an alleged offence before conducting an arrest without a warrant. Before 2005, officers could only arrest someone without a warrant if they were suspected of committing a serious offence. Now officers can arrest those they suspect of committing any crime without a warrant when it is necessary.

POLICING SPOTLIGHT

The section 24 PACE necessity test states when a person can be arrested. Jenny Sprag leaves Tesco in Bullshire having failed to pay for a bag of groceries; she is stopped by security guards and is verbally aggressive towards them and hits one of the security guards. PC Gough arrives, and Jenny Sprag is seen to punch one of the security guards in the face. She then says, '*I am going to come back and hit you again once this is finished with.*' When asked for her details, Jenny refuses to give an address. She is arrested and conveyed to the police station.

REFLECTIVE PRACTICE 3.2

LEVEL 5

Jenny Sprag has committed a number of offences. Evaluate the scenario and consider what part of the necessity test would be used to explain the reason for arrest.

ARREST PROCEDURE

As a police officer, when utilising your powers of arrest you must follow the following procedure.

- Identify yourself as the police.

- Tell the suspect that they are being arrested.

- Tell the suspect the ground of the arrest (what crime is suspected).

- Explain why it's necessary to arrest you (necessity test).

- Explain that the suspect is detained and not free to leave.

- If the person is under 18, they should not be arrested in educational premises unless unavoidable and a parent or guardian should be informed as soon as possible upon arrival at the police station.

POLICE CAUTION

On completion of the above procedure, the police caution is to be given to all persons arrested at the time of arrest. An exception to this rule is if it is impracticable because of their condition or behaviour at the time. If it has not been possible to give the caution at the time of arrest, it is to be completed as soon as the person is able to comprehend the caution. The caution is necessary to ensure that the suspect's rights are protected and that the possible consequences of saying or not saying anything are fully understood

There are two main versions of the caution: the 'when questioned caution', in section 10.5, PACE Code C, is given upon arrest, where there are grounds to suspect someone of an offence and they must be cautioned before being asked any questions about the offence and at any subsequent point when questioned, namely at the beginning of interviews.

The 'when' caution is broken down into the following three elements.

1. 'You do not have to say anything' – the suspect does not have to say anything that may incriminate themselves and may remain silent.

2. 'But it may harm your defence if you do not mention when questioned something which you later rely on in court' – if the suspect is charged to court and if during the court hearings they introduce information that they did not mention during the investigation, the court can choose how much notice to give to it.

3. 'Anything you do say may be given in evidence' – anything said during the investigation from arrest will be recorded and may be heard in court.

The alternative is the 'now caution', found in section 16.2 of PACE Code C, that is usually given at the end of an investigation if the person has been charged with or informed that they may be prosecuted for an offence.

The 'now' caution is also broken down into three elements, as follows.

1. 'You do not have to say anything.'

2. 'But it may harm your defence if you do not mention now something which you will later rely on in court.'

3. 'Anything you do say may be given in evidence.'

Can you see the difference? If so, why do you think there is a difference? See Figure 3.1 for an example of the full caution process.

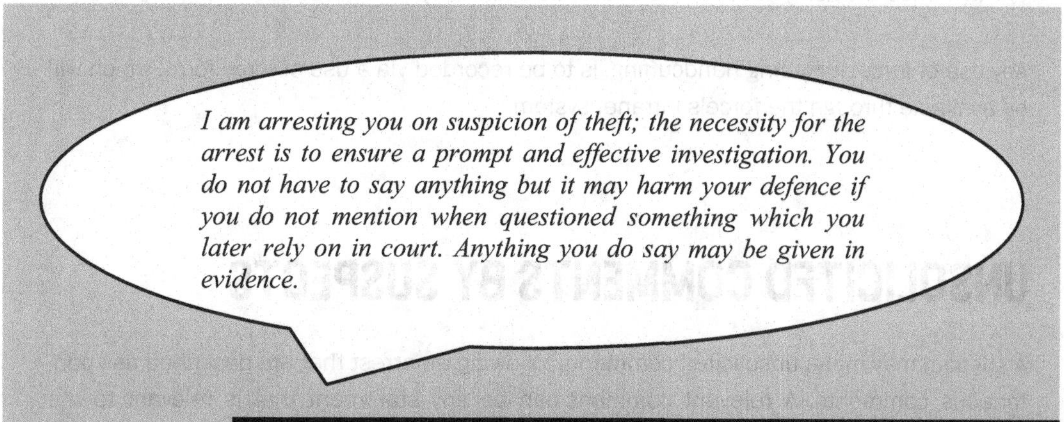

> *I am arresting you on suspicion of theft; the necessity for the arrest is to ensure a prompt and effective investigation. You do not have to say anything but it may harm your defence if you do not mention when questioned something which you later rely on in court. Anything you do say may be given in evidence.*

Figure 3.1 An example of an arrest and caution of a suspect for theft

REASONABLE FORCE TO EFFECT AN ARREST

In order to effect an arrest, officers may use reasonable force as stated in section 3 of the Criminal Law Act 1967; section 117 of the Police and Criminal Evidence Act 1984 and common law. Reasonable force has previously been mentioned in Chapter 2 on stop and search. The meaning of 'reasonable' in this context is as follows:

- absolutely necessary for a purpose permitted by law;

- the amount of force used must also be reasonable and proportionate (ie the degree of force used must be the minimum required in the circumstances to achieve the lawful objective); otherwise, it is likely that the use of force will be excessive and unlawful.

Any excessive use of force is unlawful, and officers found to have used excessive force face disciplinary action, which could include arrest and imprisonment.

For clarity, section 76(7) of the Criminal Justice and Immigration Act 2008 sets out the following considerations when deciding if the force used is responsible, which have been adopted from case law:

- that a person acting for a legitimate purpose may not be able to weigh to a nicety the exact measure of any necessary action;

- that evidence of a person having only done what the person honestly and instinctively thought was necessary for a legitimate purpose constitutes strong evidence that only reasonable action was taken by that person for that purpose.

Any use of force, including handcuffing, is to be recorded via a use of force form, which will be available through the force's intranet system.

UNSOLICITED COMMENTS BY SUSPECTS

A suspect may make unsolicited comments following an arrest that are described as spontaneous comments. A relevant comment can be any statement that is relevant to the offence (Code C, para 11.13 and note 11E, PACE 1984). For example, such a statement could be '*it wasn't my fault, he asked for it*'.

Such comments are to be recorded in an officer's pocket notebook and recorded in direct speech with the time the statement was made and signed by the officer, and if practicable by the suspect. If the suspect does not agree with the comment, then their rationale should be recorded and a signature requested.

POWER TO SEARCH ON ARREST

Upon arresting a suspect other than in a police station, a police officer has a power to conduct a search of the person and any premises they were in at the time of arrest. This might also include where they were immediately prior to the arrest if they were arrested for an indictable offence, a power afforded by section 32 of PACE. To search the premises, the officer must reasonably believe that the premises may contain evidence, and must only search to the extent that is reasonably required to discover any such item or evidence

Section 18 of PACE gives additional powers to search following an arrest. This allows an officer to enter and search the premises occupied or controlled by a suspect who has been arrested for an indictable offence; however, there must be reasonable grounds for suspecting that evidence relating to the offence or similar offences are present. Authority must be sought from someone at inspector level or above in writing. However, such authority is not needed if the arrested person is present, for the effective investigation of the offence, but an officer of the rank of inspector must be advised on completion of the search.

RECORDING THE ARREST

Upon arresting a suspect, the following details are required to be recorded in your pocket notebook:

- time of arrest;

- reason for arrest;

- place of arrest;

- unsolicited comments.

These details are required when booking the person into custody, which is discussed later. When recording the information within your notebook, the mnemonic **ELBOWS** should be followed:

- **E** – no erasures;
- **L** – no leaves torn out/no lines missed;
- **B** – no blank spaces;
- **O** – no overwriting;
- **W** – no writing between lines;
- **S** – statements in 'direct speech'.

The following activities will allow you to consider this.

REFLECTIVE PRACTICE 3.3

LEVEL 4

- Consider the police caution. Which caution would you use when arresting a suspect – 'when' or 'now'?

- What details must you record when arresting a person?

CRITICAL THINKING ACTIVITY 3.2

LEVEL 6

- Critically analyse the following statement and question.

It has been argued that the caution is too complicated and on occasions not used correctly. Is there a need to simplify the police caution so those arrested understand their rights? What would you suggest?

DETENTION OF A SUSPECT

Following the arrest of a suspect, the person is to be taken to a designated police station and booked into custody. Upon arrival at the police station the following information is required by the custody sergeant:

- time of arrest;

- place of arrest;

- circumstances of the arrest (reasoning behind the arrest and the criminal act);

- necessity test (PACE 1984, s.24).

It is for the custody sergeant to decide if the person shall be authorised to be detained or released. If detention is authorised, then the person will be booked into custody and you will be required to assist with this procedure, such as recording the suspect's belongings and conducting further searches of the person to ensure they are safe to be detained. It is imperative that all information known about the suspect is recorded to consider any risk they may be to themselves or others while in custody to prevent and injury or death. In order to ensure that people are detained safely within custody, the custody sergeant will refer to PACE Codes C and G and the safer detention and handling of persons in police custody guidance (ACPO, 2012).

POWERS TO DETAIN

Parts IV and V of PACE provide the police with powers to detain those they have arrested without charge. The detention of a suspect is often crucial to a police investigation. Once detained, the police have powers to question the suspect and collect their biometric information such as DNA under sections 63 and 63A of PACE and Code D. The information collected during detention can help the police determine whether a suspect should be charged with a criminal offence.

The detention of a suspect under PACE is subject to strict time limits. The police should deal with suspects 'expeditiously' and release them 'as soon as the need for detention no longer applies'. Most suspects can only be detained without charge for up to 24 hours. Individuals arrested for serious offences may be detained without charge for up to four days if authorised by senior officers and the courts under sections 42 and 43 of PACE.

The police should aim to make a charging decision while the suspect is in custody. Suspects who cannot be charged are normally released 'under investigation' but they can be 'bailed' when it is proportionate and necessary to do so.

Section 37(2) of PACE allows the custody officer to release the suspect, having determined that there is currently insufficient evidence to charge them. The suspect may be released pending the obtaining of further evidence – with bail where the pre-conditions for bail are satisfied or without bail (release under investigation) where the pre-conditions for bail are not met.

When bail is granted, conditions of bail can be attached where necessary to prevent the suspect from:

- failing to surrender;

- offending on bail;

- interfering with prosecution witnesses;

- otherwise obstructing the course of justice;

- or for their own protection.

Suspects released on bail may be required to report to the police at regular intervals while the investigation is ongoing, or be subject to other controls designed to protect victims and witnesses or preserve evidence.

- Doorstep condition – to enforce a curfew or a residence condition imposed for one of the statutory purposes.

- Not to drive.

- Sureties.

- Electronic tagging.

- Electronic tagging with GPS location monitoring.

While a suspect is in custody or on bail they can be 'ruled out' of the crime due to further investigations. The police should notify those that have been arrested but are no longer under investigation as soon as practicably possible and release them without delay.

PACE Code C provides statutory guidance on police detention powers. Police forces are required to detain people held under PACE in accordance with the code. The College of Policing has published authorised professional practice guidance on detention and custody. His Majesty's Inspectorate of Prisons (HMIP) and His Majesty's Inspectorate of Constabulary and Fire & Rescue Services (HMICFRS) have published responsibilities for police custody. They measure police forces against these expectations during their regular inspections of police custody facilities.

FURTHER ACTIONS OF THE ARRESTING OFFICER

Once a suspect has been accepted into custody by the custody sergeant, you must use this time effectively in your investigation to continue with investigation strategies, which are discussed in a later chapter.

You are required to write an arrest statement which should include all relevant details of the arrest on form MG11. The statement should include a full description of the offender for identification purposes. Guidance for identification was set out in case law, namely *R v Turnbull* [1976] Cr App R 132 (note for students – when discussing case law *R v* is said as 'Crown and') using the mnemonic **ADVOKATE**.

- **A**mount of time the suspect was under observation.
- **D**istance between the witness and suspect.
- **V**isibility (lighting, day or night, weather conditions etc).
- **O**bstructions between suspect and witness.
- **K**nown or seen before.
- **A**ny reason for remembering the suspect.
- **T**ime lapse between the first and any subsequent identification.
- **E**rrors between the first recorded description and the suspect's actual appearance.

POLICING SPOTLIGHT

Having completed this chapter, reconsider the scenario from page 18.

PC Jones is out on night foot patrol in the city centre. At his briefing session he was informed by his sergeant that there has been a high number of night-time burglaries in the city centre. PC Jones sees Sam Smith, a local boy who was known to him from previous dealings with him and other members of their family. PC Jones approaches Smith and asks him where he has been and where he was going. Smith does not reply.

PC Jones starts to search Smith, who objects and pushes away PC Jones. Smith is arrested but not told why he has been arrested before and he is not cautioned. On arrival at the police station, PC Jones conducts a search of Smith and locates ten packets of cigarettes.

Smith is accepted into custody and placed in a cell. PC Jones decides to go and search the home address of Smith although he has not sought any authority to conduct this search. Upon arrival, PC Jones is refused entry by the father of Smith. PC Jones forces entry and searches the premises and finds several unpacked computers. PC Jones arrests Mr Smith.

REFLECTIVE PRACTICE 3.4

LEVEL 4/5

Consider and comment on the actions of the officer in relation to the following.

• The legality of the arrest. What details must PC Jones provide Smith and record?

• The legality of the second search.

• The legality of the search of Smith's home and the property recovered; what authority could PC Jones request?

• The scenario refers to Sam Smith as a local boy, suggesting he is under 18. Who should be informed as soon as reasonably possible?

• What information should be given to Mr Smith upon his arrest?

As a police officer you have a responsibility to ensure that you are always acting in compliance with legislation and following the correct procedures; the above scenario would have allowed you to consider the failings of PC Jones. The failings of PC Jones could lead to the case being thrown out of court as the evidence would be inadmissible and therefore the victims of the crime would feel they have been let down by the police.

SUMMARY OF KEY CONCEPTS

This chapter has discussed the powers of arrest and detention. The following key concepts were considered.

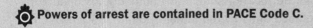 **Powers of arrest are contained in PACE Code C.**

Officers must record all details of the arrest.

Officers are to record all subsequent statements by the suspect after arrest in their pocket notebook in direct speech and have the suspect sign them.

- Police officers may use reasonable force to effect an arrest but it must be reasonable and justified.

- Police powers and policing interact with each other.

CHECK YOUR KNOWLEDGE

1. How many powers of arrest are there?

2. How many versions of the police caution are there?

3. How long can a person be detained with an extension authorised by the court?

4. What code within PACE covers the necessity test?

5. What power of search is used to search after arrest?

Sample answers are provided at the end of this book.

FURTHER READING

BOOKS

Bryant, R and Bryant, S (2021) *Blackstone's Handbook for Policing Students.* Oxford: Oxford University Press.
Chapter 10 of this book discusses police powers and an officer's duties.

Newman, T (2005) *Handbook of Policing.* Abingdon: Willan Publishing
This book concentrates on the role of a police officer and covers the duties of a police officer.

WEBSITES

College of Policing (2022) APP (Authorised Professional Practice). [online] Available at: www.app.college.police.uk (accessed 6 October 2022).
The College of Policing APP web pages provide a searchable resource, covering guidance on many aspects of police powers.

Police and Criminal Evidence Act 1984 [online] Available at: www.legislation.gov.uk/ukpga/1984/60/contents (accessed 6 October 2022).
This site provides further reading on the Police and Criminal Evidence Act 1984.

CHAPTER 4
DISPOSALS OF SUSPECTS

LEARNING OBJECTIVES

AFTER READING THIS CHAPTER YOU WILL BE ABLE TO:

- detail various disposal methods of suspects;

- understand the information required to conduct disposals;

- describe the procedures to conduct disposals;

- explain the use of various police powers.

INTRODUCTION

As a police officer there is a need for you to understand the various disposal decisions available for offenders. These are a fundamental part of the criminal justice system. Such decisions can be made by the police or the Crown Prosecution Service (CPS) and are referred to as charging decisions (a person attends court) or out-of-court disposals. Section 37A of the Police and Criminal Evidence Act 1984 states that the Director of Public Prosecutions may issue guidance for the purposes of enabling custody officers to decide how people should be dealt with. This can be either by court or an out-of-court disposal defining who can make the decisions, either the police or the CPS. The disposal decisions are made in line with policing strategies and partner strategies to obtain a shared picture of the threat and risks to communities by sharing information. The aim of this is to:

- protect the vulnerable;

- prevent further offending;

- provide early intervention with potential offenders;

- provide partnership working to assist with reducing crime.

To ensure that there is a national strategic aim for the delivery of disposal methods, the National Police Chiefs Council created the 'Charging and Out of Court Disposals: A National Strategy 2017–2021' (Glen, 2016). This chapter will discuss in court and out-of-court disposals and the role police officers play in the decision-making process. The following activities will assist you in developing these skills.

REFLECTIVE PRACTICE 4.1

LEVEL 4

- In the previous chapter we discussed the arrest of Sam Smith for the theft of cigarettes. Would it be beneficial to send Sam Smith to court or are there other ways to prevent his offending?

CRITICAL THINKING ACTIVITY 4.1

LEVEL 4

- Critically analyse the following statement and question.

Sam Smith has been arrested and is awaiting further investigation of the offence; he is a first-time offender. It has been argued that first-time offenders, depending on their offence, should always be given a second chance to dissuade them from continuing in a life of crime. Is this the right course of action?

OUT-OF-COURT DISPOSALS

An out-of-court disposal is the method of finalising an investigation without the need for the person to attend court. There are numerous methods of out-of-court disposal that need to be discussed so that a clear understanding of them can be obtained. The out-of-court disposals are as follows:

- no further action;

- restorative justice;

- community resolution;

- cannabis warning;

- penalty notice for disorder;

- youth caution (under 18);

- adult caution;

- youth conditional caution (under 18);

- adult conditional caution;

- foreign national offender conditional caution.

Each area is now discussed.

NO FURTHER ACTION

With any investigation there can come a point where it is proven that the person detained is not responsible for the offence and that person will be released with no further action. However, persons can be released with no further action on advice from the CPS; this is usually when there is not enough evidence for a prosecution to take place. When this occurs you need to advise the detained person that they are being released with no further action and this should be completed in writing by the custody sergeant and recorded on the custody recording system. You must advise the detained person that they should retain any documents or evidence that supports their defence as the investigation can be resumed if fresh evidence comes to light or new or historical allegations are made which are relevant to the investigation. In essence, the person is released from custody pending any further lines of inquiry coming to light; should this happen, the person would be rearrested.

RESTORATIVE JUSTICE

Restorative justice is the term given to a process where the offender makes amends for the criminal acts they have committed. Restorative justice is facilitated by a trained officer or volunteer and brings the victim and offender together in a controlled environment if they agree to take part. The meeting holds the offender accountable to both the victim and the community where the harm has been caused. This gives the suspect the opportunity to make amends for their behaviour. Restorative justice is also beneficial to the victim as it has been shown to bring them closure on the incident and places them at the centre of the process. The use of restorative justice has been shown to reduce reoffending and help to divert offenders away from the criminal justice system. Restorative justice can be utilised to avoid a criminal conviction. More information is available via the Restorative Justice Council website where testimonies from victims and offenders prove the worth of the scheme.

COMMUNITY RESOLUTION

Community resolutions are a non-statutory disposal method which can include elements of restorative justice and are used when it is proportionate to deal with low-level crimes such as low-cost theft, minor criminal damage, minor assault with no injuries and anti-social behaviour. Community resolutions are administered by the police. There is a need for the offender to accept responsibility for their behaviour and to take part in a community resolution, which usually occurs when the victim of the crime agrees and does not want more formal action taken. Such resolutions can reduce the chance of the person reoffending as they have taken responsibility for the harm caused. Resolutions can include advice on their behaviour, a letter of apology to the victim, and some form of reparation such as repairing the damage or paying for this to be done.

When deciding if a community resolution is proportionate, the following topics should be considered.

- **Actual offence** – based on the circumstances of the offence, it must be in the public interest to offer a community resolution.

- **Evidential standard** – it must be clear that a crime or incident has occurred, and there is reasonable suspicion that the offender is responsible.

- **Admission of guilt** – the offender must accept responsibility for the offence.

- **Offender consent** – the offender must agree to participate in community resolution and be capable of understanding the situation and process.

- **Offender history** – the offender should have no relevant offending history. If they have previously offended, the police officer should refer the decision to a supervisor and record the reasons for the decision.

- **Victim check** – the victim(s) should be consulted and agreement sought. A community resolution can proceed without victim consent, but the supervisor must agree to the decision and the rationale should be recorded.

- **Implications** – a community resolution does not form part of a criminal record, but it may be disclosed in an enhanced Disclosure and Barring Service (DBS) check.

It is important when administering a community resolution order that the offender accepts responsibility for the offence and that they understand the full process and implications of accepting the resolution. The police officer must ensure that all relevant paperwork such as a crime report are completed for the offence and all relevant policies and procedures within the officer's force are met. While the offender accepts responsibility for their actions, they are not burdened by a criminal record, and evidence has shown that the reoffending rates are reduced (Restorative Justice Council, 2016). Community resolutions can be used for both youth and adult offenders. Community resolution administrative considerations include the following.

- Confirm that the offender accepts responsibility for the offence.

- Explain the process to the offender.

- Explain how the offender will rectify the harm.

- Explain to the offender the implications of receiving a community resolution.

- Ensure the community resolution is recorded appropriately.

Now consider the following policing spotlight scenario.

POLICING SPOTLIGHT

James Brown is found to have committed criminal damage to several garden gnomes by smashing them with a stick. The homeowner is aware that James is 15 years old and does not have a criminal record. It is reported that James committed the act while acting up in front of a number of friends. The homeowner, Mrs Shaw, does not want to see James receive a criminal record and asks for an alternative resolution. James fully admits the offence and apologises for his actions. He promises to rectify the harm he has caused to Mrs Shaw by agreeing to cut her grass for two weeks. The whole process of community resolution is explained to James, and he agrees to take part. James completes the tasks and therefore does not receive a criminal record and is now aware of the harm he caused. Mrs Shaw is also happy, as she can see that James is remorseful and has completed the order.

CANNABIS WARNING

In 2004, cannabis warnings were introduced for those found to have simple possession of cannabis. Simple possession is regarded as a small amount of cannabis for personal use. Cannabis remains a controlled Class B drug under the Misuse of Drugs Act 1971. In order to tackle this low-level crime of simple possession, a three-stage escalation procedure was introduced. An offender would receive a cannabis caution for their first possession offence, a penalty notice for disorder (discussed later in this chapter) for their second, and would be arrested for a third possession. The officer should give a verbal warning to the offender at a police station or in the street; the warnings only apply to those over the age of 18 at the time of the possession. No more than one warning can be administered per offender. It is important to note that any warnings issued after 26 January 2009 must be taken into account when deciding the intervention level. Those prior to this date should be considered as previous offending history.

When deciding if a cannabis warning is proportionate, the following considerations should be taken into account.

- **Actual offence** – is the possession of a small amount of cannabis consistent with personal use?

- **Evidential standard** – the police officer must have reasonable suspicion that an offence of cannabis possession has been committed and there is sufficient evidence for a realistic prospect of conviction.

- **Admission of guilt** – the offender must make a clear and reliable admission of all elements of the offence.

- **Offender consent** – the offender is not required to explicitly consent to accepting the cannabis warning.

- **Offender history** – the offender must be aged 18 years or over, with no evidence of dealing or possession with intent to supply. The offender must not be smoking cannabis in the company or vicinity of young or vulnerable people. They should not have raised a defence to the offence, must be able to understand what is happening, be compliant with the warning procedure, possess a verifiable name and address and have no previous record of a cannabis warning, penalty notice for disorder or drugs convictions.

- **Implications** – the cannabis is confiscated and a record of the cannabis warning is made on local systems. Cannabis warnings can be placed before the court for use as evidence of bad character and may also be disclosed as part of an enhanced DBS check, if deemed relevant.

POLICING SPOTLIGHT

CANNABIS WARNING ADMINISTRATIVE CONSIDERATIONS

- Confirm that the offender admits the offence.

- Explain the process to the offender, highlighting that any further offending is likely to result in a penalty notice for disorder or arrest, as they cannot receive multiple cannabis warnings.

- Explain to the offender the implications of receiving a cannabis warning, ie it does not form part of a criminal record, but a record will be made on local systems.

- Ensure the cannabis warning is recorded appropriately.

→

Unlawful possession of cannabis is a notifiable crime which must be recorded in accordance with the National Crime Recording Standard (NCRS) and the Home Office Counting Rules for Recorded Crime (HOCR) for crime. The crime should be recorded as 'detected by way of cannabis warning', in accordance with local policy.

PENALTY NOTICE FOR DISORDER

Penalty notice for disorder (PND) was established by the Criminal Justice and Police Act 2001 and is a statutory disposal method. PNDs are often referred to as a financial punishment to manage low-level anti-social and nuisance offending. PNDs can be administered in the street or at a police station. They can only be issued to persons over the age of 18 for 29 specified offences, including:

- being drunk and disorderly in a public place;

- retail theft under £100;

- behaviour likely to cause fear, alarm or distress;

- criminal damage (up to a value of £300) and cannabis possession.

A PND also has an option for the offender to attend an educational course relating to the offence which they must pay for, known as a PND-E. Once completed, their liability to pay the ticket is discharged; however, they can opt to pay the ticket in full and not attend an educational course. With both a PND-E and a PND the offender has the right to request a court hearing. There are two levels of fines of £60 and £90; once issued, the recipient has 21 days to pay the penalty or request a court hearing. The following is an example of the procedure in given situations.

- If the recipient pays the penalty within 21 days of receipt, they discharge all liability for the offence.

- If the recipient requests a court hearing within 21 days, the case will be reviewed by a crown prosecutor, who will apply the evidential and public interest test under the Code for Crown Prosecutors.

- The offender may opt to attend an educational course related to the penalty offence. The individual must either book themselves on a course or be contacted by a course provider within 21 days. They must pay for the course in advance or on the day, and complete the course in order to discharge their liability.

- If the course is not booked or completed within a locally agreed timescale, the fine is 150 per cent of the original penalty offence and is enforced by the courts in the usual way.

- If the recipient fails to respond within 21 days, a fine of 150 per cent of the original penalty value will be registered against them and enforced by the magistrates' court.

When issuing a penalty notice for disorder, the following operational considerations should be taken into account.

- **Actual offence** – PNDs may be issued for 29 penalty offences only, where the offence is not too serious.

- **Evidential standard** – the officer must have reasonable suspicion that a penalty offence has been committed and that sufficient evidence can be obtained to support a successful prosecution.

- **Admission of guilt** – this is not required. Accepting a PND is not an admission of guilt.

- **Offender consent** – explicit consent is not required but a PND should be issued to, and received by, the offender.

- **Educational course** – checks should be carried out to determine whether the force area has opted to run a relevant course. It is not mandatory and the chief officer decides whether or not to provide such an option.

- **Offender history** – the offender must be aged 18 years or over, have a verifiable address, be able to understand what is happening, and be compliant. The offending history should be assessed and a PND considered an appropriate disposal.

- **Victim check** – views should be sought and recorded, as a PND disposal removes the possibility of the criminal court awarding a compensation order in favour of the victim.

- **Implications** – a crime record is created as a result of a PND.

A police officer should carry out the following actions once a PND is given.

- Explain the PND process to the offender, including how they should pay the penalty, request a court hearing or choose the educational option, as well as the consequences of not paying or requesting a court hearing.

- Explain the implications of receiving a PND to the offender:

  o   it does not form part of a criminal record but a crime record will be created;

  o   it will show as an outcome on the police national computer (PNC) and may also be disclosed as part of an enhanced DBS check if deemed relevant;

  o   it may also be cited as evidence of bad character in subsequent criminal proceedings and relied on as evidence at court in civil proceedings, for example, Anti-Social Behaviour Order (ASBO) applications.

- Ensure the PND is recorded appropriately. Where the offence relates to a notifiable crime, a crime report must be completed. The recording of the offence and the subsequent detection must be carried out in accordance with the NCRS and HOCR for crime.

CRITICAL THINKING ACTIVITY 4.2

LEVEL 5

- Having discussed the use of penalty notices, consider and critically analyse the following statement and question.

The introduction of penalty notices has given offenders the opportunity to avoid a criminal record. Could it be argued that the introduction of the Penalty Notice for Disorder has moved away from the principles of the rule of law, namely for the accused to face their day in court?

YOUTH CAUTION

The Legal Aid, Sentencing and Punishment of Offenders Act (LASPO) 2012 introduced youth cautions which can be given for any offence, but are intended for low-level crime. The decision to give such a caution is made by the police, but the young offender must be referred to a youth offending team (YOT) if this is the second out-of-court disposal. However, if the police have concerns about the offender, they may refer them at the first out-of-court disposal. The YOT will work with the young offender to deter them from committing further offences. If the offence is an indictable offence, then CPS authorisation is required prior to the delivery of the youth caution.

When considering suitability for a caution, it must be appropriate, namely the offender's attitude, type of offence (utilising the ACPO gravity matrix) and effectiveness of the caution to prevent reoffending must be taken into account. A youth caution does not have to be disclosed to an employer but may form part of an enhanced DBS check. It should also be noted that if the offender has been dealt with in court for an offence and would have been subject to the sex offenders register the same registration requirements would apply.

When deciding to give a caution the following considerations should be taken into account.

- **Actual offence** – based on the circumstances of the offence, including any aggravating factors, it must be in the public interest to offer a caution instead of prosecution.

- **Evidential standard** – there must be sufficient evidence to meet the standard for a realistic prospect of conviction.

- **Admission of guilt** – the offender must admit the offence and there must be sufficient evidence for a realistic prospect of conviction. However, a youth caution can only be given if it is not in the public interest to prosecute.

- **Offender consent** – provided the offender continues to admit the offence, they do not have to expressly accept a youth caution if it is determined to be the most appropriate disposal for the offence committed.

- **Offender history** – offenders must be between 10 and 17 years of age, inclusive. Any previous offending history and willingness to engage with interventions should also be considered at the decision-making stage.

- **Victim check** – the views of the victim must be considered in determining the seriousness of the offence, although the final decision to use the youth caution remains with the police.

- **Implications** – youth cautions form part of a criminal record. They are considered spent at the time that they are given but may be disclosed in future criminal proceedings.

POLICING SPOTLIGHT

CONSIDERATIONS FOR DELIVERY OF A YOUTH CAUTION

- Explain the process to the recipient.

- Explain the implications of receiving a youth caution.

- Confirm that the offender admits the offence.

- Ensure the youth caution is recorded.

- Arrange to have an appropriate adult present.

ADULT CAUTION

Adult cautions can be administered for any offence. They are intended for low-level offending and are permitted to caution for summary and either-way offences (summary offences and either-way offences are offences that can be heard in a magistrates' court and are usually for lower-level crime); the exceptions are as follows:

- possession of a bladed article, offensive weapon or firearm in public, including threatening with a bladed article or offensive weapon in a public place or a school;

- child prostitution and pornography, cruelty to a child, indecent images of children;

- supplying Class A drugs.

As a formal warning, the adult offender must have admitted the offence and it is a non-statutory disposal when it is not in the public interest to prosecute the offender. Any caution for an indictable offence must be referred to the CPS and be authorised by a superintendent. An adult caution is determined according to its appropriateness in relation to the offender, the offence and the likelihood of it being effective in preventing reoffending.

The following requirements are needed to validate a caution:

- admission of guilt by an offender over 18 years of age;

- sufficient evidence available for a realistic prospect of conviction;

- proof that it is not in the public interest to prosecute the offender;

- agreement of the offender to accept the caution.

Suitability for an adult caution is determined according to its appropriateness in relation to the offender, the offence and the likelihood of it being effective at preventing reoffending. When considering an adult caution, the adult offender gravity matrix should be used to decide if an adult caution is appropriate; the matrix is available on the police national legal database (PNLD).

The following must be completed when issuing an adult caution.

- **Actual offence** – based on the circumstances of the offence and including any aggravating factors, it must be in the public interest to offer a caution instead of prosecution.

- **Evidential standard** – sufficient evidence is needed for a realistic prospect of conviction.

- **Admission of guilt** – the offender must admit to committing the offence.

- **Offender consent** – the offender must be able to understand and explicitly consent to accepting the caution.

- **Offender history** – the offender must be 18 years or over, be willing to accept a caution and not raise a defence to the offence. Any previous offending history should be assessed to ensure the outcome is appropriate. In addition, exceptional circumstances must be present if a caution is being considered for a repeat offender. If they have been cautioned for a similar offence within a two-year period, the decision must be authorised by a senior police officer.

- **Victim check** – the victim should be consulted, and their views sought. They do not, however, have the right to insist on a specific outcome.

- **Implications** – adult cautions form part of a criminal record and may be disclosed in some circumstances in future legal proceedings or to an employer, as part of a standard or enhanced DBS check. If the caution is administered for sexual offences, the offender may be placed on the sex offenders register and/or prevented from working with children and vulnerable adults.

POLICING SPOTLIGHT

Arthur Stanley is a 39-year-old male who had been arrested for theft of a loaf of bread and a packet of ham. He has no previous convictions and has fully admitted the offence. He is eligible for an adult caution. He has made a full and frank admission to the offence during interview and is remorseful for his actions. The custody sergeant agrees that in the circumstance he may receive a police caution, which is approved by the duty inspector. The duty inspector informs Arthur of the implications of the caution and instructs PC Wright to ensure that the relevant paperwork has been submitted.

Remember that there is a need to confirm the following actions are completed for the administration of an adult caution.

- Explain the process to the offender.

- Explain the implications of receiving an adult caution.

- Confirm that the offender admits the offence.

- Ensure that the caution is recorded appropriately.

YOUTH CONDITIONAL CAUTION

Youth conditional cautions are a youth caution with conditions attached and must be appropriate, proportionate and achievable. The conditional cautions must be:

- reparative – can include apologising to the victim, paying compensation or making good any damage;

- rehabilitative – can include attendance at treatment courses;

- punitive – fines for damage and unpaid work (only used when the reparative and rehabilitative conditions are not suitable or sufficient for the offence committed).

Youth conditional cautions are available for any offence; however, indictable offences must be referred to the CPS. They are intended for low-level crimes and are used when it is not in the public interest to prosecute. The ACPO gravity matrix should be used to access the offender's suitably for the caution; in all cases, the offender should be referred to the YOT for mandatory assessment. Once this assessment is completed, the police and the YOT decide on the best conditions to attach; the young offender must agree to the conditions or they cannot be offered. Any condition attached must be for a period of three months only and compliance will be monitored by the YOT.

The following operational considerations must be adhered to when issuing a youth conditional caution.

- **Actual offence** – youth conditional cautions may only be offered for an offence set out in CPS (2013b) the *Director's Guidance on Youth Conditional Cautions*. They are not generally suitable where, if prosecuted, the offender would be likely to receive a substantial community order or imprisonment.

- **Evidential standard** – must have sufficient evidence to meet the standard for a realistic prospect of conviction, where it is ascertained that the public interest would be best served by the offender complying with suitable conditions rather than undergoing a formal prosecution. In this case, a youth conditional caution should be considered an appropriate disposal to reduce reoffending and make reparation for harm caused.

- **Admission of guilt** – the offender must admit to committing the offence.

- **Offender consent** – the offender must explicitly accept the conditional caution and the conditions attached.

- **Offender history** – offenders must be between 10 and 17 years of age, inclusive. Any previous offending history and willingness to engage with interventions should also be considered at the decision-making stage. The youth must then be referred to the YOT to be assessed.

- **Victim check** – the victim should be consulted and their views sought. They do not, however, have the right to insist that the matter is disposed of in a particular way. If appropriate, a victim can be awarded compensation or reparation.

- **Implications** – failure to comply with the conditions attached to a youth conditional caution can result in prosecution for the original offence. A youth conditional caution forms part of a criminal record, but is spent as soon as the conditions are complied with. Normally, the caution would not need to be disclosed to an employer. It may, however, form part of an enhanced DBS check if this is considered appropriate.

If the young offender complies with the youth conditional caution then no further action is taken.

ADULT CONDITIONAL CAUTION

An adult conditional caution is a statutory disposal with conditions attached in line with the youth conditional caution, namely reparative, rehabilitative or punitive, and was introduced by the Criminal Justice Act 2003. Adult conditional cautions can be issued for all summary offences and common either-way offences, but not including motoring offences. Offences for which such a caution can be given are listed in the *Director's Guidance on Adult Conditional Cautions* (7th ed) (CPS, 2013a). The police have the power to issue the cautions but they must be referred to the CPS by an officer of the rank of inspector. Such cautions are spent after a three-month period.

Adult conditional cautions are not suitable when the offender is likely to receive a substantial community order or imprisonment. When deciding to administer an adult conditional caution, the following should be taken into account.

- **Evidential standard** – there must be sufficient evidence for a realistic prospect of conviction, where it is ascertained that the public interest is best served by an offender complying with suitable conditions rather than being prosecuted.

- **Admission of guilt** – the offender must admit to committing the offence.

- **Offender consent** – the offender must be likely to accept the caution and explicitly consent to the conditions.

- **Offender history** – the offender must be 18 years or over and be willing to comply with the conditions. Any previous offending should be assessed, and a conditional caution dispensed only if considered appropriate to modify offending behaviour or make reparation for harm caused.

- **Victim check** – the victim should be consulted and their views sought. They do not, however, have the right to insist that the matter is disposed of in a particular way. If appropriate, a victim can be awarded compensation or reparation.

- **Implications** – if the conditions are not complied with or the offender withdraws from the caution, the offender may be prosecuted for the original offence. A conditional caution forms part of a criminal record and may, in some circumstances, be disclosed in future proceedings or to an employer when applying to work with children and vulnerable adults. This is as part of a DBS check.

POLICING SPOTLIGHT

Police officer actions when completing an adult conditional caution.

- Explain the process to the offender.

- Explain the implications of receiving a conditional caution.

- Confirm that the offender admits the offence and is willing to comply with the conditions.

- Ensure the conditional caution is recorded appropriately.

FOREIGN NATIONAL OFFENDER CONDITIONAL CAUTION

The foreign national offender conditional caution is designed to allow foreign nationals to receive police cautions, as further discussed in this section. Introduced by the Legal Aid, Sentencing and Punishment of Offenders Act 2012 (LASPO), this conditional caution must be rehabilitative such as attending a treatment centre or reparative such as apologising to the victim, paying compensation or repairing any damage. The primary caution is one that requires the individual to leave the country, co-operate with authorities and not return to the UK for five years; these conditions must be appropriate, proportionate and achievable. Foreign national offender conditional cautions are available for all summary and either-way offences with a penalty of up to two and a half years of imprisonment. Offences that such a caution can be given for are listed in the *Director's Guidance on Adult Conditional Cautions* (7th ed) (CPS, 2013a). Further information is available in the Criminal Justice Act 2003 (Conditional Cautions: Code of Practice) Order 2013. An officer of the rank of sergeant can authorise the caution for summary and triable either-way offences but any indictable offences must be referred by an inspector to the CPS.

The following considerations should be take into account when deciding to administer such a caution.

- **Actual offence** – conditional cautions may only be offered for an offence set out in the *Director's Guidance on Adult Conditional Cautions* (7th ed) (CPS, 2013a).

The police officer must take note of the different offence types applicable to a foreign national offender conditional caution, which relate to the penalty for the offence being up to two-and-a-half years' imprisonment.

- **Evidential standard** – there must be sufficient evidence for a realistic prospect of conviction, where it is ascertained that the public interest is best served by an offender complying with suitable conditions rather than being prosecuted.

- **Admission of guilt** – the offender must admit to committing the offence.

- **Offender consent** – the offender must be likely to accept the caution and explicitly consent to the conditions.

- **Offender history** – the offender must be 18 years or over, must be able to be removed from the country on the authority of the UK Border Agency, and be willing to comply with the conditions of the caution. Any previous offending should be assessed, and a conditional caution dispensed only if considered appropriate to modify offending behaviour or make reparation for harm caused. If the offender claims asylum, or there are reasonable grounds for believing that the offence committed is connected to human trafficking, then a conditional caution cannot be used.

- **Victim check** – the victim should be consulted, and their views sought. They do not, however, have the right to insist that the matter is disposed of in a particular way. If appropriate, a victim can be awarded compensation or reparation. The victim is entitled to legal advice for both the criminal and immigration matter.

- **Implications** – if the conditions are not complied with or the offender withdraws from the caution, the offender may be prosecuted for the original offence. The conditions will include leaving the country, complying with the authorities and not returning to the country within five years. If they fail to comply, the case will be returned from the UK Border Agency to a force single point of contact (SPOC) for consideration, and the offender may be prosecuted for the original offence, or the conditions varied.

- **A conditional caution** forms part of a criminal record and may, in some circumstances, be disclosed in future proceedings or to an employer when applying to work with children and vulnerable adults. This is as part of a DBS check.

POLICING SPOTLIGHT

Police officer actions when completing a foreign national offender conditional caution.

- Explain the process to the offender.

- Ensure that the offender can understand what is being said and that they use an interpreter if necessary.

- Explain the implications of receiving a conditional caution, including the significance of the admission of guilt, the ban from the UK and criminal record implications.

- Confirm the offender admits the offence and is willing to comply with the conditions.

- Ensure the conditional caution is recorded appropriately.

EVIDENCE-BASED POLICING

THE EFFECTIVENESS OF OUT-OF-COURT DISPOSALS

The use of out-of-court disposals within the criminal justice system has been described as a 'caution culture' with victims reporting that they feel there are no real consequences for the offenders and that the system allows offenders to walk away scot-free (*Police Professional*, 2014, p 7). It could therefore be argued that while the system benefits the criminal justice system by reducing the number of offenders appearing before a court, it is felt there is no real conclusion for the victim, who feels that they have not had a satisfactory resolution to the offence committed. Therefore, there is a need for continued research into the effectiveness of out-of-court disposals. Such research was conducted by Neyroud and Slothower (2015), who examined the effectiveness of the programmes to ascertain if the assertions by the victims were correct and if out-of-court disposals were effective. Such findings can be used to develop the systems to ensure the out-of-court disposals remain beneficial to society on a whole and continue to meet the needs of the criminal justice system, the victim and the offender. In turn, this can aid the development of the disposals available to the courts. This in essence is evidence-based practice in action.

IN-COURT DISPOSAL

When an offender has been arrested and the investigation has been completed, you must consider all relevant out-of-court disposals. Once these are rejected, you will seek a charging decision from the Crown Prosecution Service (CPS). A charging decision is when the CPS are requested to view the available evidence and decide on what offences the detained person should be charged with. This is achieved by completing an advice file and presenting this to the CPS, who will decide if there is enough evidence to charge the person with the offence and will also give recommendations regarding the likelihood of bail. The Bail Act 1976 stipulates when bail can be considered and the actions to be taken when bail is refused. When bail is granted, the offender can be released with or without conditions. The conditions can include not to attend or contact certain areas or people prior to appearing in court; sureties can also be requested such as surrendering their passport or reporting to a police station every day prior to the court case. If bail is refused, the offender is charged but remains in custody to appear at the next available magistrates' court for a hearing to decide if bail can be granted; these are known as remand court hearings. The first appearance for any defendant will be at the magistrates' court where decisions will be made regarding whether a trial is needed at a magistrates' court or if the case needs to be heard at a Crown Court.

REFLECTIVE PRACTICE 4.2

LEVEL 4

- Consider the out-of-court disposals outlined in this chapter, which are varied and wide. Do you think that more emphasis is placed on out-of-court disposals to reach a speedy solution for the victim?

CRITICAL THINKING ACTIVITY 4.3

LEVEL 5

- Consider the following statement and critically evaluate the question.

Since the Covid-19 pandemic it has been argued that the criminal justice system is failing. Can it be argued that with so much energy given to out-of-court disposals that the government have recognised this and are therefore pushing out-of-court disposals to reduce the stress on the criminal justice system or is it a balanced approach?

POLICING SPOTLIGHT

Consider the scenario from pages 18 and 51.

Sam Smith and his father are in custody following their arrests by PC Jones.

The investigation into the alleged theft of cigarettes has been completed and it is discovered that Sam Smith had purchased the cigarettes at a local shop on behalf of his mother. He admits to pushing the officer and accepts this was wrong and apologises. While Sam is known to the police, he has no previous convictions or cautions.

Mr Smith admits that he refused to give the police entry as he believed they did not have the power to enter his home and no explanation was given by the officers when they attended. Mr Smith has several previous convictions, most of them theft related but has no police cautions.

The officer investigating the case, PC McDonald, has reviewed all the evidence and seeks your advice on the disposal of both parties.

REFLECTIVE PRACTICE 4.3

LEVEL 4/5

Consider the following.

- What out-of-court disposal is available for Sam Smith?

- In regard to Mr Smith, would it be right to close the case with no further action?

- Does Sam Smith have to agree to take part in the out-of-court disposal?

SUMMARY OF KEY CONCEPTS

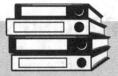

This chapter has discussed disposal of suspects and explored the following key concepts.

- Out-of-court disposals are varied.

- LASPO is the Legal Aid, Sentencing and Punishment of Offenders Act 2012.

- Offenders must agree to taking part in restorative justice actions and conditional cautions.

- Youth out-of-court disposals relate to persons 17 years of age and younger.

- Youth offending teams work in partnership with the police to deter offenders from reoffending.

CHECK YOUR KNOWLEDGE

1. Can you refuse to take part in a conditional caution?

2. How many out-of-court disposals have been discussed?

3. How many cannabis warnings can a person be given?

4. If a foreign national conditional caution is issued, how long must the person not return to the UK?

5. What does LASPO stand for?

Sample answers are provided at the end of this book.

FURTHER READING

BOOKS

Hemmens, C, Brody, D C and Spohn, C (2021) *Criminal Courts: A Contemporary Perspective*, 5th edition. London: Sage.

WEBSITES

Association of Chief Police Officers (2012) Guidelines on the Use of Community Resolutions (CR) Incorporating Restorative Justice (RJ). [online] Available at: https://library.college.police.uk/docs/appref/Community-Resolutions-Incorporating-RJ-Final-Aug-2012-2.pdf (accessed 6 October 2022).

Crown Prosecution Service (2019) *Conditional Cautioning: Youths – DPP Guidance*. [online] Available at: www.cps.gov.uk/legal-guidance/conditional-cautioning-youths-dpp-guidance (accessed 6 October 2022).
This website provides information about conditional cautions.

Crown Prosecution Service (2022) *Conditional Cautioning: Adults – DPP Guidance*. [online] Available at: www.cps.gov.uk/legal-guidance/conditional-cautioning-adults-dpp-guidance (accessed 6 October 2022).
This website provides information about conditional cautions.

Legal Aid, Sentencing and Punishment of Offenders Act (LASPO) 2012 [online] Available at: www.legislation.gov.uk/ukpga/2012/10/contents/enacted (accessed 6 October 2022).
The Legal Aid, Sentencing and Punishment Act 2012.

Ministry of Justice (2013a) *Code of Practice for Youth Conditional Cautions*. [online] Available at: www.gov.uk/government/publications/code-of-practice-for-youth-conditional-cautions (accessed 6 October 2022).
This website provides information about conditional cautions.

Ministry of Justice (2013b) *Simple Cautions: Guidance for Police and Prosecutors*. [online] Available at: www.gov.uk/government/publications/simple-cautions-guidance-for-police-and-prosecutors (accessed 6 October 2022).
This website provides information about adult cautions.

Ministry of Justice (2014) *Penalty Notices for Disorder: Guidance for Police Officers.* [online] Available at: www.gov.uk/government/publications/penalty-notices-for-disorder-guidance-for-police-officers (accessed 6 October 2022).
This website provides information about penalty notices.

Police and Criminal Evidence Act 1984 [online] Available at: www.legislation.gov.uk/ukpga/1984/60/contents (accessed 6 October 2022).
The Police and Criminal Evidence Act 1984.

Restorative Justice Council (2011) *ACPO Restorative Justice Guidance and Minimum Standards.* [online] Available at: https://restorativejustice.org.uk/resources/acpo-restorative-justice-guidance-and-minimum-standards (accessed 6 October 2022).
This website provides guidance on the community resolutions and restorative justice.

Restorative Justice Council (2016) *Restorative Justice and Policing – What You Need to Know.* [online] Available at: https://restorativejustice.org.uk/sites/default/files/resources/files/rjc-policeandrj-5digi.pdf (accessed 6 October 2022).
This website provides guidance on the community resolutions and restorative justice.

Youth Justice Board for England and Wales (2013) *Youth Cautions: Guidance for Police and Youth Offending Teams.* [online] Available at: www.gov.uk/government/publications/youth-cautions-guidance-for-police-and-youth-offending-teams (accessed 6 October 2022).
This website provides information about youth cautions.

CHAPTER 5
THE PEACE MODEL AS AN INVESTIGATIVE STRATEGY

LEARNING OBJECTIVES

AFTER READING THIS CHAPTER YOU WILL BE ABLE TO:

- ⚙ describe the PEACE model;

- ⚙ understand the importance of building rapport with a suspect;

- ⚙ explain the importance of an investigative mindset free of bias;

- ⚙ comprehend the use of various police powers.

INTRODUCTION

This chapter discusses the PEACE model of investigation. It is important for an investigator to keep a clear and open mindset, free of bias, to ensure that all areas of the investigation are covered. Bias can lead to inaccurate interpretations of information and material, which in turn can lead to the unfair treatment of people and the ultimate failure of any investigation. Impartiality is core to a good investigation of crime. In any investigation there is a need to maintain accurate records of the management of the investigation, which incorporates various elements from searches to interview. The investigation process and further strategies are discussed in the *Criminal Investigation* title of this series but this chapter will concentrate on the interviewing of witnesses and the use of the PEACE model.

The PEACE model was introduced in 1992 and is used by various government departments when there is a need to interview a suspect or witness, and by the police forces of England and Wales (Walsh and Bull, 2010). It is described as an interviewing technique rather than an interrogation of the persons interviewed. The structure of PEACE leads itself to allow the person being investigated to discuss the incident and to seek their version of what occurred (Walsh and Bull, 2010). Other techniques are used in other parts of the world, namely the Reid model or Reid Technique of Interviewing and Interrogation, which is a registered trademark of John Reid and Associates Inc, developed in 1974. This technique is used by over 500,000 law enforcement agencies, mainly in the US. The Reid model is based on the interrogation of the suspect, and it is argued that it has led to numerous false confessions. A similar style was used during the investigation of the Birmingham Six and the Guildford Four. These cases involved the investigation of suspected IRA bombers, who all confessed to the crime under interrogation but were later found to be innocent of the crimes. Since these notable cases, a more reliable technique for interviewing was needed and this saw the birth of the PEACE model.

REFLECTIVE PRACTICE 5.1

LEVEL 4

As discussed in previous chapters, the Police and Criminal Evidence Act (PACE) 1984 details how a person detained by the police should be treated.

- Considering that suspects have the right to silence during interview, which of the above techniques would you identify as the best to make a suspect talk, or is there even a need to get the suspect to talk?

CRITICAL THINKING ACTIVITY 5.1

LEVEL 5

- Consider the following statement and critically evaluate the question.

The Reid model has been criticised for leading to false confessions by suspects, but the police have used the PEACE model since 1992. Why is it that suspects still make false confessions?

PEACE MODEL OF INTERVIEWING

The PEACE model is divided into five separate stages, each as important as each other. None of the stages should be missed to ensure that the interview is conducted as effectively as possible. The PEACE model stages are as follows.

- **P**lanning and preparation.

- **E**ngage and explain.

- **A**ccount clarification and challenge.

- **C**losure.

- **E**valuation.

When interviewing a suspect, it is important to ensure that PACE Code C is complied with, and that the suspect has the right to silence and legal representation during the interview. Even if the suspect indicates that they will not respond to any of the questions put to them, there is still a need to follow the five stages as at some point the suspect may wish to say something. When interviewing a suspect, it is quite common to be put off by the suspect remaining silent or reciting '*no comment*' throughout an interview but remember that this is their opportunity to tell their version of events, and the court may consider the fact that they failed to discuss their version of events when given the opportunity to do so.

This chapter will now consider each stage of the model in order.

PLANNING AND PREPARATION

Prior to any interview you will need to plan and prepare, and take account of all available information, identifying the key issues and objective of the interview. This is required even if you need to conduct an early interview. During the planning stage, you will need to create an interview plan highlighting the areas you wish to discuss and the evidence to hand, practical arrangements such as who will be present and what room will be used, as well as if the suspect has a legal representative or appropriate adult if needed. This stage allows the interviewer to review the investigation, know what evidence is to hand and decide on the aims and objectives of the interview.

When considering the interview plan, the interviewer must be mindful that the material obtained helps to establish the accuracy of the matter under investigation and there is a need to consider the answers carefully. The following are some questions you should consider when preparing the plan.

- Who needs to be interviewed and in what order?

- Why is a particular interviewee's viewpoint so important?

- What information should now be obtained?

- Should the interviewee be interviewed immediately, or would it be more useful to wait until more information has been obtained about the circumstances of the offence from other sources?

When planning interviews there is a need to consider some of the following areas with regard to the interviewee.

- **Age** – knowing the interviewee's age to decide whether an appropriate adult/ interview supporter is required.

- **Cultural background** – this can affect the way a person prefers to be addressed, and may also indicate the need for an interpreter.

- **Religion or belief** – eg interviewers may need to take prayer requirements into account.

- **Physical and mental health** – knowledge of an existing medical condition and ensuring that appropriate facilities are used.

- **Disability** – this refers to any condition that makes it more difficult for a person to do certain activities or have equitable access to the world around them. Disabilities may be cognitive, developmental, intellectual, mental, physical, sensory or a combination of multiple factors. Disability can be from birth or acquired during a person's lifetime.

- **Previous contact with the police** – this helps to determine factors such as the interviewee's reaction and the interviewer's safety.

When planning for the interview, several practical arrangements also need to be considered that may help the interviewer understand the offences under investigation.

- **Visiting the scene** – enables the interviewer to understand the layout of where the incident took place.

- **Searching relevant premises** – have all searches been conducted? Are any outstanding?

- **Location of the interview** – is there available space and is it practicable to accommodate all present? (interview team/suspect/legal representative/ appropriate adult/interpreter)

- **Role of interviewers** – who will be the lead and who will take notes/assist?

- **Timings** – how much time is left on the PACE clock, how long should the interview last, is there a need for breaks?

- **Equipment** – does all the equipment work?

- **Exhibits and property** – are they available? Are they needed for the first interview?

- **Knowledge of the offence** – do you understand the offence? Do you understand the points to prove?

The plan for the interview should be in written form and can be used as an aide throughout the interview. It should contain the elements listed, which will prove a good starting point and can be further developed. You can also include planning for a 'no comment' interview or a planned prepared statement from the suspect or read by the legal representative, introduction of significant comments made on arrest or since and/or silences. If there is more than one interviewer, it is important to plan each person's role, such as note-taking, so that each interviewer understands their role, and both can conduct the interview without obstructing the other. A good plan before an interview will lead to a professional and organised interview, allowing you to follow all stages of the PEACE model. The following reflective practice will develop your skills.

REFLECTIVE PRACTICE 5.2

LEVEL 4

- Consider the scenario previously discussed. You are tasked with interviewing Sam Smith following his arrest. Write a plan to interview Sam from the available information.

ENGAGE AND EXPLAIN

This step is broken down into two areas: engage and explain. The engage section is probably the most important as it is important to engage with the interviewee and encourage a conversation. This is described as rapport building and can be commenced as soon as meeting the suspect and engaging in small talk encouraging the interviewee to become involved in a conversation. However, you must not question the interviewee until you commence the interview or caution the interviewee. There is a need to ensure that, when engaging with the interviewee, active listening is used to listen to the answers. This will prepare you for the interview, where there is a need to ensure that you actively listen to all responses given as this may assist you during the interview and helps to maintain rapport. Once the interview has commenced, rapport building and active listening can be demonstrated by communicating interest in the interviewee's account; this will assist you in identifying important evidential information.

Upon beginning the interview there is a need to explain the process to the interviewee and clearly explain why the person is there, such as 'you were arrested on suspicion of...' and what you will be discussing in the interview: 'During this interview I am going to be discussing the events of last night and in particular the events leading up to your arrest.' It is good practice to explain to the interviewee that should they make any non-verbal comments such as shaking of the head, that you will explain this action to the tape but that you would encourage the interviewee to verbalise any responses. It is also worthwhile explaining that during the interview, notes will be taken and who will be taking them. It is also worthwhile explaining to the interviewee that they will not be interrupted but you may ask questions to clarify what they have said, as this will remind you to listen to their account without interruption.

ACCOUNT CLARIFICATION AND CHALLENGE

The third part of the PEACE model is the account clarification and challenge stage. During this stage the interviewer should use open and non-leading questions to assist the interviewee in giving an accurate account. The use of open questions enables the interviewee to give longer answers rather than yes or no, as is often the case when using closed questions. A typical opening gambit by police officers when interviewing is *'so tell me what happened'*. This allows the interviewee to give their account and follow-up open questions can be asked. The 5WH guide is a useful technique for asking open questions.

- What happened?

- Where did it happen?

- Why did it happen?

- When did it happen?

- Who was there?

- How did it happen?

To encourage the interviewee to continue to speak, you should continually use active listening skills and verbal indications such *'ok'*, *'thanks'* and *'carry on'* to demonstrate that you are listening. It is also important to ensure you give the interviewee time to pause and recall the events from memory without interruption.

Once the account has been given, you should clarify what has been said. This is accomplished by breaking the account down into manageable topics and probing the account that has been given. At this point, closed questions may be used to clarify a point, such as *'it was 10 o'clock when you left your house?'* This can be continued until the fullest picture of the person's account can be obtained, covering information that has not been covered in your planning phase.

The questions used should be kept as short and simple as possible without any police jargon, other language or complicated words the interviewee may not understand. It is good practice to avoid multiple questions as they can confuse the interviewee and lead to a full account not being achieved. Forced-choice questions should also be avoided, such as *'was it a saloon or an estate car?'* With this type of question, the interviewee is likely to choose a response rather than suggest an alternative such as *'hatchback'*. As previously discussed, the interviewer should avoid leading questions as they imply the answer or assume facts, and the interviewee is unlikely to dispute them. The responses from such questions are likely to be less credible and could be ruled inadmissible in a court of law. The best interviews are ones that feel like a conversation about the incident and the interviewer is able to obtain material (evidence) that is useful to the case.

When planning for the interview, you would have identified several topics to be discussed at interview; this can be completed in one interview or several interviews. Only once all the topics have been covered and the interviewee has given their account is there the opportunity to challenge the account given. This is completed by demonstrating to the interviewee the evidence you must hand over to challenge the said account and once again allowing them to respond to the challenges. It is important that all topics have been covered and the interviewee has been allowed to give their account before a challenge is put in because challenging too early could lead the interviewee to stop engaging with the process and to simply refuse to answer any questions. Challenging an interviewee is an area that takes practice and challenges should be planned within the first phase of the PEACE model. The following reflective practice will assist you in this area.

REFLECTIVE PRACTICE 5.3

LEVEL 4

Consider the following types of questions that could be used during an interview. Record what they mean to you and when they should or should not be used.

- Open-ended.

- Specific closed.

- Forced choice.

- Multiple.

- Leading.

CLOSURE

The closure stage is used to close the interview in a standard way. It is important to ensure that the closure section of the interview is planned and structured to ensure that all the information has been gathered and does not end abruptly. You should summarise the interview with time afforded to the interviewee to clarify any areas of the summarisation. Allow time for this to be completed so that it is not rushed. The interviewer should record the time and date of the conclusion of the interview. Once the interview is concluded and any recording stopped, the interviewer should explain to the interviewee what will happen next.

EVALUATION

It is important that any interviewer evaluates the interview that has taken place in order to determine if any further action is required and to ascertain how the account obtained fits with the investigation and if there is now enough evidence to charge the suspect or bail them so that further investigation can take place. The evaluation of an interview can be conducted in either written form or verbally; however, it is best practice to record all decision making. Part of the evaluation phase is also dedicated to a self-reflection period to assist the officer to develop their skills and continue to improve for future interviews.

PEACE MODEL AND WITNESS INTERVIEWS

The PEACE model is effective for interviewing suspects and witnesses and the skills developed when interviewing are just as important when interviewing victims, as they are also witnesses to the offence. The PEACE model will allow the interviewer of the witness to obtain as much information as possible, which will be recorded on a witness statement and will also assist in other records of the crime such as crime reports as they need to obtain accurate and reliable information. It is important to note that witnesses may be suffering from shock or trauma from the event and so there is a need to be sensitive and impartial to the event. Interviews should be conducted as soon as possible after the event, but if this is not possible it should be arranged at the earliest opportunity. A brief account should be recorded and signed by the witness; this can be completed in a pocket notebook if an alternative is not available such as a MG11 witness statement. Consideration should also be given to finding assistance for the witness or signposting them to support agencies. Once the interview has been conducted, the interview should be recorded on a MG11 witness statement and the witness asked to sign the paperwork. Whenever completing an interview or witness statement, there is a need to obtain the best evidence possible to complete an effective and exhaustive investigation, as demonstrated in Figure 5.1.

Achieving best evidence	PEACE
Planning and preparation	Planning and preparation
Establishing rapport	Engage and explain
Initiating and supporting a free narrative account questioning	Account, clarify and challenge
Closing the interview	Closure
Evaluation	Evaluation

Figure 5.1 Links between obtaining best evidence and the PEACE model (College of Policing, 2014)

POLICING SPOTLIGHT

You have previously considered the search and arrest of Sam Smith and subsequently his father. They have been in custody now for ten hours while you have conducted your investigation. The custody sergeant is asking when you will be ready to interview; PC Jones has gone off duty and there is a need to prepare for the interview. You should also consider that Sam is 16 years old and is eager to be interviewed.

REFLECTIVE PRACTICE 5.4

LEVEL 4/5

- What practical arrangements do you need to consider for the interview?

- What are the points to prove for the offence?

- Do you have enough information to complete the interview?

- What action can you take to gather further information before commencing the interview?

EVIDENCE-BASED POLICING

DEVELOPMENT OF THE PEACE MODEL

As discussed in this chapter, there is a need to understand the different strands of investigation and the development of strategies to resolve incidents. The PEACE model has been utilised to allow police officers to interview witnesses and offenders to assist in obtaining evidence for the offence that has been committed. However, the skills of evidence-based practice should be used to evaluate if this model of interviewing is as successful as when introduced. Ray Bull has led the way in developing the model and other academics have researched its effectiveness and made various recommendations to ensure that the model continues to be effective. Research in this area has shown that officers need adequate training and to continue to practise all elements of the model to ensure effective interviews are conducted. Evidence-based practice highlights areas that the College of Policing can advise forces on where areas of improvement can be found (Walsh and Milne, 2008).

SUMMARY OF KEY CONCEPTS

This chapter has discussed the PEACE model of interviewing and explored the following key concepts.

- The five stages of the PEACE model.

- The investigation strategy of interviewing.

- Comparison between the PEACE model and the Reid model.

- The PEACE model can be used to interview suspects as well as witnesses.

- The aim of the interview is to seek the interviewee's account of an incident.

CHECK YOUR KNOWLEDGE

1. How many parts are there to the PEACE model?

2. What types of question should the interviewer use?

3. List five practical arrangements to be considered before interview.

4. When was the PEACE model introduced?

5. What were the two cases that led to miscarriages of justice that resulted in the introduction of the PEACE model?

Sample answers are provided at the end of this book.

FURTHER READING

BOOKS

Stainton, I and Ewin, R (2022) *Criminal Investigation*. St Albans: Critical Publishing. The book provides an insight into the investigation of crime.

WEBSITES

College of Policing (2020a) *Briefing Note: Using Language Services.* [online] Available at: https://library.college.police.uk/docs/college-of-policing/Language-Services-v1.0.pdf (accessed 6 October 2022).
This website discusses the use of language services.

College of Policing (2020b) *Interpreting. Briefing the Interviewee: Aide Memoire for Interpreter-Assisted Interviews.* [online] Available at: https://library.college.police.uk/docs/college-of-policing/Briefing_the_interviewee_aide_memoire_v1.0.pdf (accessed 6 October 2022).
This website is an aide memoire to assist with using language services.

College of Policing (2020c) *Interpreting. Working with an Interpreter: Aide Memoire for Interpreter-Assisted Interviews.* [online] Available at: https://library.college.police.uk/docs/college-of-policing/Working-with-an-interpreter-v1.0.pdf (accessed 6 October 2022).
The College of Policing provides further reading on the use of interpreters.

Police and Criminal Evidence Act 1984 [online] Available at: www.legislation.gov.uk/ukpga/1984/60/contents (accessed 6 October 2022).
The website provides further reading on the Police and Criminal Evidence Act 1984.

CHAPTER 6
DISCLOSURE

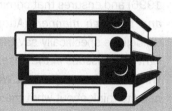

LEARNING OBJECTIVES

AFTER READING THIS CHAPTER YOU WILL BE ABLE TO:

⚙ describe what the law says about disclosure;

⚙ explain what disclosure is and its purpose;

⚙ understand to whom disclosure applies;

⚙ define the term 'material' in relation to disclosure;

⚙ understand the principles of collection and retention;

⚙ explain the differences between used, unused and sensitive material;

⚙ articulate the complexities associated with disclosure.

INTRODUCTION

Disclosure is a fundamental part of the criminal justice system. The disclosure of information by and to all parties ensures that every person has a fair trial. This right is a fundamental part of our legal system and is guaranteed by Article 6 of the European Convention on Human Rights (ECHR).

Disclosure is contained within the Criminal Procedure and Investigations Act 1996 (CPIA 1996) and ensures that criminal investigations and trials are conducted in a *'fair, objective and thorough manner'* (Attorney General's Office, 2022, p 3). The Attorney General's Guidelines specifically say that *'disclosure should be completed in a thinking manner, in light of the issues in the case, and not simply as a schedule completing exercise'* (*R v Olu, Wilson and Brooks* [2010] EWCA Crim 2975, [2011] 1 Cr. App. R. 33 [42]–[44]). Prosecutors need to think about what the case is about, what the likely issues for a trial are going to be and how this affects the reasonable lines of inquiry, what material is relevant, and whether the material meets the test for disclosure.

Until 25 years ago there was little formal regulation of this subject but since the enactment of CPIA 1996, disclosure has become the *'battleground of the modern criminal justice system'* (Ormerod, 2003, p 102).

This chapter explores what the law says about disclosure and its purpose, who it applies to and a greater understanding of the terminology. At the end of the chapter, you should be able to demonstrate an understanding of the complexities associated with disclosure

KEY PRINCIPLES OF DISCLOSURE

There are a number of important principles outlined in the Attorney General's Guidelines (2022) (see Figure 6.1).

Why is understanding disclosure important to you as an investigator? There are two primary reasons. Firstly, so that you understand the key changes to the Attorney General's Guidelines on Disclosure and the CPIA Code of Practice. Secondly, so that you apply both the Code of Practice and Guidelines to your investigations and disclosure decisions.

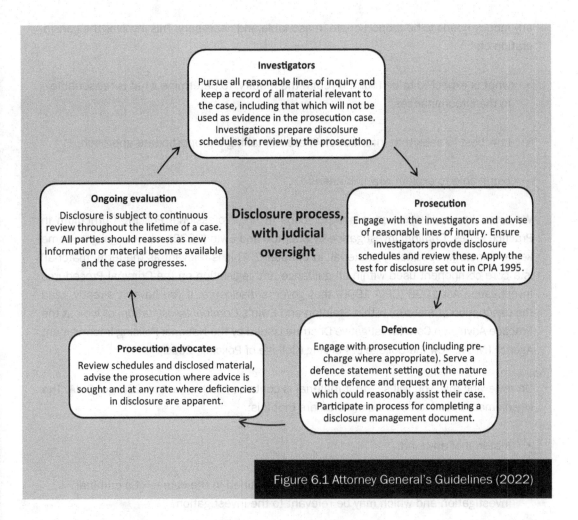

Figure 6.1 Attorney General's Guidelines (2022)

Within this context, investigations are key, and specifically the question 'what is an investigation?' We know there are three main types of investigation.

1. Investigations into crimes that have been committed.

2. Investigations whose purpose is to ascertain whether a crime has been committed, with a view to the possible instigation of criminal proceedings.

3. Investigations which begin in the belief that a crime may be committed, with a view to the possible instigation of criminal proceedings.

The principal aim of an investigator is to ensure that they are fair, and when conducting an investigation the investigator should pursue all reasonable lines of inquiry, whether these point towards or away from the suspect and may extend to material in the hands of a third party. What is reasonable in each case will depend on the particular circumstances, but any inquiry needs to be proportionate, reasonable and necessary. This involves the consideration of:

- what is expected to be found through the inquiry, to determine what is reasonable in the circumstances;

- how best to seek that information/material, taking a proportionate approach;

- being able to explain why it is needed.

We have discussed this within another book in the Professional Policing Curriculum in Practice series, *Criminal Investigation* by Stainton and Ewin (2022), which highlights some key terminology, specifically 'material' in Chapter 2. This is relevant as the term 'material' is a core component used within all guidance and legislation on the Criminal Procedures Investigation Act 1996 (CPIA 1996) that governs disclosure. If you haven't already, read the description of material within Stainton and Ewin's *Criminal Investigation*, or look at the Practice Advice on Core Investigative Doctrine issued by the National Policing Improvement Agency (NPIA), now the College of Policing (College of Policing, 2021).

On reviewing this, you will see that material is contained within section 23(1) of CPIA. The key elements used to describe material are that it is:

- material of any kind;

- includes information and objects that are obtained in the course of a criminal investigation and which may be relevant to the investigation.

The understanding of material in the context of CPIA is important as this relates to disclosure and the need to disclose all information (subject to some processes and constraints) to the defence. This includes the legal requirement contained within section 3(1) of CPIA that requires the prosecutor to:

(a) disclose to the accused any prosecution material which has not previously been disclosed to the accused and which might reasonably be considered capable of undermining the case for the prosecution against the accused or of assisting the case for the accused, or

(b) give to the accused a written statement that there is no material of a description mentioned in paragraph (a).

As has been said, the importance of disclosure and the principles attached to it is central to fairness in our criminal justice system. Getting it right matters to defendants, complainants and the public interest in criminal prosecutions (Attorney General's Office, 2022). Miscarriages of justice, flowing from disclosure failures and the resulting loss of liberty, are wrong. There is a balance to be achieved in disclosure to stop it becoming a bureaucratic disaster and derailing trials that would otherwise come to a satisfactory conclusion.

As investigators you are also committed to the European Convention of Human Rights (ECHR). As part of this requirement, there is a need to balance between the right to a fair trial (Article 6, ECHR) and the right to private and family life (Article 8, ECHR). In some instances, the investigator may need to request and/or process personal or private information, and as such impinge on another person's Article 8 rights. It is therefore imperative that investigators do so lawfully and appropriately, following the correct rules of disclosure to prevent a case collapsing.

As early as 1865 in *R v Puddick* the courts ruled that counsel for the prosecution are to regard themselves as ministers for justice, not a struggle for a conviction. This is a point sometimes overlooked in our adversarial court system.

TO WHOM DOES DISCLOSURE APPLY?

As you know, the Criminal Procedure and Investigations Act (CPIA) was introduced in 1996. It sets out clear expectations as to the requirement to disclose relevant material that either undermines the prosecution case or assists the defence in their case (s.3(1)).

The prosecutor has a statutory duty to disclose unused material to the accused that is primarily triggered by:

- *a plea of not guilty in the magistrates' court;*

- *the sending for trial at the Crown Court;*

- *the preferment of a voluntary bill of indictment, or;*

- *the service of the prosecution case following the sending of an accused to the Crown Court under section 51(1) Crime and Disorder Act 1998.*

(CPS, 2022)

A full list is set out in section 1 of the CPIA.

It is important to recognise that disclosure is a two-way street. Section 34 of the Criminal Justice Act 2003 inserted section 6C in the CPIA, requiring the person accused to give the prosecution and the court details of any witnesses they intend to use in the trial (see para 47, *R v R and Others* [2015] EWCA Crim 1941). This is considered important, as it:

- *assists in the management of the trial by helping to identify the issues in dispute;*

- *provides information that the prosecutor needs to identify any material that should be disclosed, and;*

- *prompts reasonable lines of enquiry, whether they point to or away from the accused.*

(CPS, 2022)

There is also a requirement in the legislation for the defence to provide the outline of their case in the form of a defence statement so that further consideration can be given by prosecutors to identify any relevant issue and identify material which may require any additional disclosure. Managing disclosure is a fundamental part of an investigation and prosecution. It is essential that it is dealt with competently and fairly, with a thinking approach throughout.

Disclosure is a significant issue when it comes to the integrity of a trial. According to the Crown Prosecution Service (CPS), between January and June 2021, 1648 cases collapsed over disclosure failures. Now consider the following reflective practice and critical thinking activity.

REFLECTIVE PRACTICE 6.1

LEVEL 4

Thinking about cases that may collapse, identify what is the impact on:

a) the victim;

b) the suspect;

c) the criminal justice system;

d) the wider communities?

Sample answers are provided at the end of this book.

CRITICAL THINKING ACTIVITY 6.1

LEVEL 4

- Critically analyse the following statement.

There is no need for any case to collapse as long as the police and the prosecution follow the rules.

A sample answer is provided at the end of this book.

Now you have completed the activities, consider the following Policing Spotlight, which examines the impact of failing to disclose basic material within an investigation.

POLICING SPOTLIGHT

A 28-year-old man is charged with being drunk and disorderly in a public place following a night out with a group of friends. The MG6C (the schedule of relevant non-sensitive material, see page 103) does not contain CCTV footage from the council that would have covered the scene.

The defence serve a defence statement and request the CCTV footage, explaining that it would show the defendant did not display any signs of drunkenness at all. The prosecution inform the defence that the CCTV footage will be brought to court. However, on the day of the trial, the prosecutor does not have the CCTV footage. He confirms that it exists, but it has not been reviewed and that the officer in the case (OIC) has stated that it is a format that cannot be viewed on laptops without special software.

The defence counsel explain to the magistrate that the CCTV footage should have been on the unused schedule and the prosecutor's admission that it had not been reviewed means that the prosecution had not complied with their disclosure obligations and so cannot proceed with the case.

The prosecutor then asked the defence counsel if she is making an application to adjourn. The defence counsel replies that it should be the prosecution's application, not the defence's, and that the defence is opposed to an adjournment. The prosecution point out that this is in fact the first time the case has been listed for trial and that it is in the interests of justice to grant the adjournment in order to review the CCTV material.

The prosecution application is refused, the court noting that it should have been identified within the schedule on the MG6C. The prosecution ultimately offer no evidence, being unable to comply with their disclosure obligation.

TERMINOLOGY

Correct terminology is an area of ambiguity and causes great concern in what evidence is and what does not have to be disclosed. It is important that you know what is meant when discussing disclosure. This section will look at some key terms used in disclosure.

THE DISCLOSURE TEST

The disclosure test is set out in section 3(1)(a) of the Criminal Procedure and Investigations Act 1996 and refers to the prosecutor's duty to disclose to the accused:

> *any prosecution material which has not previously been disclosed to the accused and which might reasonably be considered capable of undermining the case for the prosecution against the accused or of assisting the case for the accused.*

There is further discussion of the disclosure test later in the chapter.

MATERIAL

Material obtained in a criminal investigation, which may be relevant to the investigation, must be retained; it is not an excuse to say it was disposed of and therefore cannot be produced.

To assist, material may be photographed, video-recorded, captured digitally or otherwise retained in the form of a copy rather than the original at any time:

- *if the original is perishable;*

- *the original was supplied to the investigator rather than generated by them and is to be returned to its owner, or;*

- *the retention of a copy rather than the original is reasonable in all the circumstances.*

(CPS, 2022)

When conducting an investigation, an investigator should always have in mind their obligation to retain and record all relevant material as identified within the CPIA Code paragraphs 4 and 5 (Gov.uk, 2022).

Material which is presumed to meet the test for disclosure, as set out later in the chapter, must always be retained and recorded. All relevant material must be retained, whereas non-relevant material does not need to be retained.

RELEVANT MATERIAL

Material may be relevant to an investigation if it appears to an investigator, the officer in charge of an investigation or to the disclosure officer that it 'has some bearing on any offence under investigation or any person being investigated, or on the surrounding circumstances of the case, unless it is incapable of having any impact on the case' (Gov.uk, 2022, para 2). It is this definition, and the interpretation of it, which is resulting in significant amounts of unused material being retained to no material effect.

The issue of relevance is especially important where an investigator is considering whether:

- to throw something away;

- to return an item to the owner;

- not to record information;

- or where not keeping material or not recording information would result in the permanent loss or alteration of the material (as with reusable control room tapes, shop videos etc).

CATEGORIES OF MATERIAL FOR DISCLOSURE

In any criminal case, material subject to disclosure can be divided into two categories.

1. **Used** – this consists of statements and exhibits relied upon by the prosecution in support of its case and served on the defence.

2. **Unused** – this is an area of contention, as the officer in the case makes a subjective assessment about whether material is used or unused. Unused material is material 'which may be relevant to an investigation and which does not form part of the prosecution case' (CPS, 2022). The police must supply the CPS with any material which could be considered capable of undermining the prosecution case. Often the quantity of unused material is significant in the investigation, although the investigation should have examined all material to assess its value; on occasions, this has not happened, for example R v Allan 2016.

There are further sub-categories within the context of material and disclosure:

- **Non-relevant** – similarly, the views of the officer in the case and the subjective assessment are considered against the issues of a particular case and the material is considered as relevant or non-relevant. More detail considering relevant material is discussed later in this chapter.

- **Sensitive and non-sensitive** – they are both subject to an assessment by the officer in the case with consideration whether, if disclosed, the material would bring serious prejudice to an important public interest.

SERVED

Served means that the evidence to be used in the prosecution case has been served (given) to the defence. There can be problems within this area when there is uncertainty around what documents have been given to the defence.

OFFICER IN THE CASE

The officer in the case (OIC) is the officer who is in charge of the direction of the investigation. They also have responsibility for ensuring all procedures are conformed to.

DISCLOSURE OFFICER

In most straightforward cases, the role of the disclosure officer is undertaken by the officer in the case. This has the benefit of reducing duplication and effort. In some police forces, the duties of the disclosure officer are undertaken by crime file builders who are responsible for assimilating and collating the evidence prior to the file being submitted to the CPS. This gives consistency to the quality and content of the schedules but runs the risk that unused material might be missed and, in addition, does not assist the development and training of police officers, which can hamper them when they later come to handle more complex cases where they need to deal with unused material. It is generally only in the larger, more complex/serious cases that a specialist or dedicated disclosure officer is appointed.

PROSECUTOR

The prosecutor is the authority responsible for the conduct of criminal proceedings on behalf of the Crown.

MG6C

The MG6C is the police form setting out the schedule of relevant non-sensitive unused material. Within this form the reviewing CPS lawyer will indicate the classification of the evidence through the following ways.

- **D** – Disclose to the defence.

- **I** – Item disclosable and the defence may inspect it.

- **CND** – Clearly not disclosable (by description).

- **ND** – Document viewed and not disclosable.

MG6D

The MG6D is the police schedule of relevant sensitive material, and is not supplied to the defence. This form informs the prosecutor of the existence of relevant unused material which the disclosure officer believes should be withheld from the defence.

ROLE OF THE POLICE IN DISCLOSURE

INVESTIGATE, RECORD AND RETAIN

As investigators, the police are at the very start of the process of disclosure handling. Failure to investigate thoroughly all the evidence that points either towards or away from a suspect can result in inappropriate discontinuance or acquittal or wrongful conviction. While not equivalent, both such outcomes are ultimately miscarriages of justice.

No system of disclosure can ever prevent the fraudulent or dishonest concealment of material by a party to an investigation. However, a properly managed disclosure process, which complies fully with CPIA and other key guidance, should support a competent and thorough investigation ensuring that, wherever possible, unresolved questions are answered long before the case is put before a jury or bench of magistrates.

Consider the case below and what impact disclosure has on the outcomes.

EVIDENCE-BASED POLICING

In 1988, Lynette White was 20 years of age when she was brutally murdered in a flat in Cardiff. Stephen Miller, John and Ronald Actie, Yusef Abdullahi and Anthony Paris, who later became known as the 'Cardiff Five', were prosecuted for her murder and in 1990 three of them were convicted: Stephen Miller, Yusef Abdullahi and Anthony Paris. The case against them comprised accounts from eyewitnesses, confessions to civilians and a single recorded confession by Stephen Miller to police officers. Following the convictions, the main eyewitnesses withdrew their evidence as did most of the civilians to whom confessions were alleged to have been made. The Court of Appeal quashed the three convictions in 1992 because Miller's confession to police officers had been obtained by oppression involving bullying, hostility and intimidation.

Due to advances in DNA technology, in 2003 it was discovered from blood found at the scene that the murderer was Jeffrey Gafoor. Gafoor confessed to murdering Lynette White on his arrest and in that same year he pleaded guilty to her murder. A review of the case and the circumstances surrounding its collapse was conducted by Richard Horwell KC, who found the following, among other points.

- There was an inability of the criminal trial system to flush out disclosure issues and to bring them before the judge.

- There was too narrow a disclosure test applied.

- There was inadequate skills, training and experience of disclosure police officers (in particular, lead disclosure officers).

- There was an inability to retain disclosure officers.

- There was a lack of instruction to police officers as to how to deal with sensitive documents.

- There was insufficient formality in formulating and recording advice.

- There was a lack of appreciation of the significance for disclosure purposes of material generated within the investigation as opposed to material physically received from outside.

(The full *Mouncher Investigation Report* can be found here: https://assets.publishing. service.gov.uk/government/uploads/system/uploads/attachment_data/file/629725/ mouncher_report_web_accessible_july_2017.pdf.)

REFLECTIVE PRACTICE 6.2

LEVEL 5

- Access and read the Mouncher Report
- Consider the aspects of disclosure that you are now aware of and consider what you would have done if you had been the senior investigating officer in charge of the investigation outlined above.

DEFINITIONS

REASONABLE LINE OF INQUIRY

A reasonable line of inquiry is that which points either towards or away from the suspect. What is reasonable will depend on the circumstances of the case; there should be consideration of the prospect of obtaining relevant material and the perceived relevance of that material.

DISCLOSURE TEST

> *The test requires the prosecution to disclose to the accused any prosecution material which has not previously been disclosed to the accused and which might reasonably be considered capable of undermining the case for the prosecution against the accused or of assisting the case for the accused.*
>
> (Gov.uk, 2022, emphasis added)

The decision as to relevance requires you to make a judgement and, although some material may plainly be relevant or non-relevant, ultimately this requires a decision by the disclosure officer or investigator. As part of their role, disclosure officers and/or investigators must inspect, view, listen to or search all relevant material. The disclosure officer must provide a personal declaration that this task has been completed.

As we have discussed, there is a specific duty to retain material that may be relevant to an investigation. This duty now includes material falling into the following categories.

- *Contemporaneous records of the incident.*

- *Custody records.*

- *Incident logs.*

- *Descriptions of the offence or offender.*

- *Previous accounts made by a witness.*

- *Final versions of witness statements and drafts where the content differs.*

- *Interview records with potential witness and suspects.*

- *Material relating to other suspects.*

- *Communications between the police and experts such as forensic scientists.*

- *Expert reports and schedules of material prepared by the expert.*

- *Records of first description of a suspect.*

- *Material casting doubt on the reliability of a witness.*

(Gov.uk, 2022)

It is recognised that in some cases a detailed examination of every item of material would be disproportionate. In certain cases – primarily those involving digital material – the disclosure officer can apply search techniques. These are contained within Annex A of the Attorney General's Guidelines.

Whatever the approach taken by disclosure officers in examining material, it is crucial that disclosure officers record their reasons for a particular approach in writing.

In deciding whether material satisfies the disclosure test you should also consider the following points.

- *The use that might be made of it in cross-examination.*

- *Its capacity to support submissions that could lead to the exclusion of evidence; a stay of proceedings or a court or tribunal finding that the accused's rights under the European Convention on Human Rights had been violated.*

- *Its capacity to undermine the reliability or credibility of a prosecution witness.*

- *The capacity of the material to have a bearing on scientific or medical evidence in your case.*

- *Material relating to the accused's mental or physical health, intellectual capacity, or to any ill treatment, which the accused may have suffered when in your custody.*

(CPS, 2022)

THE REBUTTABLE PRESUMPTION

It is important to understand that the Act itself has not changed, which means that the test for disclosure has not changed.

However, both the Code of Practice (para 6.6) and the Attorney General's Guidance (paras 86–92) now state that certain categories of material will be presumed to meet that test. That presumption is referred to as the 'rebuttable presumption'.

That material will include:

- contemporaneous records of the incident;

- custody records;

- incident logs;

- descriptions of the offence or offender;

- previous accounts made by a witness;

- interview records with potential witness and suspects;

- material casting doubt on the reliability of a witness.

While you must schedule and give the prosecutor a copy of any material which has been categorised as rebuttable presumption material, that does not mean that it will automatically be disclosed to the defence.

- You should start your review of the material with a presumption that it should be disclosed to the defence. Then **apply the disclosure test in a thinking manner and consider each item of material carefully in the context of your case**. Indicate whether it is, or is not, considered to satisfy the test for disclosure and in either case explain the reasons for coming to that view.

- The prosecutor must do likewise and record their decision as to whether this type of material does or does not meet the test for disclosure, recording their reason for that decision.

CONTINUING REVIEW

This is a continuing duty on the prosecutor, for the duration of the criminal proceedings against the accused, to disclose material which satisfies the test for disclosure (subject to public interest considerations). To enable them to do this, any new material coming to light should be treated in the same way as the earlier material.

INVESTIGATION MANAGEMENT DOCUMENT

The investigation management document (IMD) will allow you to document your approach to an investigation and will include the circumstances of the case, including the issues that are likely to be contended, such as:

- any defences raised;

- pre-charge engagement;

- communication between a complainant and any other person that is relevant to the case;

- examination of mobile phones and other electronic devices;

- CCTV recovery and review;

- police body-worn video;

- social media recovery and review;

- communications data applications;

- third party material;

- forensic material;

- material meeting the disclosure test and material already disclosed;

- issues arising from the defence case statement;

- any other information that will assist the prosecutor.

The IMD will be completed for all either-way and indictable-only cases and those summary cases in the youth and magistrates' court that would benefit from an IMD due to the complexities of the case (see Attorney General's Office, 2022, para 93).

The IMD will be used by the prosecutor to complete a disclosure management document, which will set out the strategy and approach of the prosecution in relation to disclosure and will be served on the defence and the court at an early stage (see Attorney General's Office, 2022, paras 93–5 and Annex C).

DISCLOSURE MANAGEMENT DOCUMENT

Completion of a disclosure management document (DMD) by the CPS is mandatory in all Crown Court cases. Prosecutors also need to consider whether it would be beneficial in cases heard in the magistrates' court or youth court. The Attorney General's Guidelines describe the DMD as a living document intended to assist the court which will enable early engagement with the prosecution. It is most likely to be beneficial in cases with the following six features.

1. *Substantial or complex third-party material.*

2. *Digital material in which parameters of search, examination or analysis have been set.*

3. *International inquiries.*

4. *Linked operations.*

5. *Non-recent offending.*

6. *Material held or sought by the investigation that is susceptible to a claim of legal professional privilege.*

(CPS, 2022)

When you consider the below activity and have made a decision based on the information you have, reflect on the impact completing the IMD and the DMD will have on your investigation.

CRITICAL THINKING ACTIVITY 6.2

LEVEL 6

During a search of the home of a suspected paedophile, you find eight computers. Three of them are in the loft, with one each in the son's and daughter's bedrooms. One is in the downstairs lounge to which everyone in the family has access. One is in the office used by the suspect and the other is in the same office but unplugged and not being used.

Considering all aspects discussed, evaluate which computers you would seize and view, and what is your decision making for this? (Consider the case of *R v R and Others* [2015] EWCA Crim 1941.)

Sample answers are provided at the end of this book.

The requirement to ensure that disclosure officers have sufficient skills and authority relevant to the investigation is the responsibility of the appropriate chief constable. In *DS and TS* [2015] EWCA Crim 662 and *Boardman* [2015] EWCA Crim 175, it is identified that there is a personal responsibility of the chief constable (or equivalent) as well as the chief Crown prosecutor for ensuring that, among other things, police officers appointed to act as disclosure officers are trained and competent to fulfil this role and are appropriately supervised by the investigative authority.

CROWN PROSECUTION SERVICE

The Crown Prosecution Service (CPS) prosecutes criminal cases that have been investigated by the police and other investigative organisations in England and Wales. The CPS is independent, and makes its decisions independently of the police and government.

The duty of the CPS is to make sure that the right person is prosecuted for the right offence, and to bring offenders to justice wherever possible. The CPS:

- decides which cases should be prosecuted;

- determines the appropriate charges in more serious or complex cases, and advises the police during the early stages of investigations;

- prepares cases and presents them at court;

- provides information, assistance and support to victims and prosecution witnesses.

Prosecutors must be fair, objective and independent. This means that to charge someone with a criminal offence, prosecutors must be satisfied that there is sufficient evidence to provide a realistic prospect of conviction, and that prosecuting is in the public interest. They must consider whether evidence can be used in court and is reliable and credible, and there is no other material that might affect the sufficiency of evidence. Crown prosecutors must be satisfied there is enough evidence to provide a '*realistic prospect of conviction*' against each defendant.

Their role is to advise about possible reasonable lines of inquiry, evidential requirements, pre-charge procedures, disclosure management and the overall investigation strategy. Within their role they must only start or continue a prosecution when the case has passed both stages of the Full Code Test, which is when all outstanding reasonable lines of inquiry have been pursued; or prior to the investigation being completed, the prosecutor is satisfied that any further evidence or material is unlikely to affect the application of the Full Code Test, whether in favour of or against a prosecution (CPS, 2018).

The full code test has two stages:

1. the evidential stage;

2. the public interest stage.

During the evidential stage and throughout the case, prosecutors must consider the impact of disclosure and whether there is any material that may affect the assessment of the sufficiency of evidence, including examined and unexamined material in the possession of the police, and material that may be obtained through further reasonable lines of inquiry.

In every case where there is sufficient evidence to justify a prosecution or to offer an out-of-court disposal, prosecutors must go on to consider whether a prosecution is required in the public interest.

The importance of disclosure and getting it right is emphasised in the prosecutor's assessment of the case and the evidence. They will use checklists to determine the quality of the police file and consider the following points.

- What are the deadlines for initial disclosure?

- Has an initial defence letter been sent to the defence?

- Has a complete set of all MG6Cs and accompanying MGCE been provided with the brief?

- Are the MG6Cs complete or is there more material to be disclosed?

- Is there more unused material to be reviewed and what date will this be done by?

- Are the descriptions on the MG6C clear and informative?

- Are all the MG6Cs dated and signed by the disclosure officer and reviewing officer?

- Have all entries been endorsed CND or D?

- Have all the items marked disclosable been disclosed?

- Has a defence statement been dated and served?

- Does the defence statement identify the real issues of the case? If not, an adequacy statement should be raised.

- Who is the disclosure officer?

- Who is the OIC in the case?

- Has there been a written response to the defence statement?

- Have the police conducted PNC checks on all proposed defence witnesses?

- Are there any outstanding inquiries?

(CPS, 2022)

Given the complexity and the issues associated with disclosure, the impact of failing to comply with the rules governing disclosure in the below activity becomes a relevant question.

CRITICAL THINKING ACTIVITY 6.3

LEVEL 5

Critically analyse the following question.

• If we consider disclosure is about fairness, why is total disclosure of evidence not considered?

Sample answers are provided at the end of this book.

POLICING SPOTLIGHT

The defendant is in his 50s, of good character and has previously worked as a carer for old people. The allegation is that he stole nearly £10,000 from a vulnerable old man by using his bank card and PIN number over a period of two years. The issue was raised by the complainant's daughter. She reported the matter to the police saying that the money had gone missing. By then the complainant was not fit enough to provide evidence on the subject matter.

When the defendant was arrested, he immediately denied the allegation and set out in full an account that the old man had asked him to get the money for shopping and the excess balance was left in a drawer in the bedside table so that he could assist a friend who had fallen on hard times.

The defence repeatedly requested access to the social service files and reports from other carers during the relevant times. None were provided, despite the case taking a long time to be listed for trial.

On the Friday before trial, the police and CPS produced the file that the defence had been asking for. Defence counsel spent the weekend reading the files and they revealed a picture which wholly supported the defendant's account: the elderly man telling carers at the time that he had asked the defendant to obtain money for him in the approximate sums alleged so that he could assist an old friend of his who had fallen on hard times. This was confirmed by a number of independent carers and social service supervisors who queried the older man's generosity and were told that he knew perfectly well what he was doing and that he intended to carry on doing it. As a result of the late disclosure the prosecution offered no evidence.

This is another example of the impact disclosure can have on a case if the investigators do not carry out their functions in compliance with the law and guidance. During this investigation the man was arrested, charged and was about to stand trial, when the examination of material took place by the defence that highlighted the truth. This case should never have got to court, and it could be argued that if the police had undertaken their investigation thoroughly in the first instance, the man should have never been arrested.

ADDITIONAL GUIDANCE

The Attorney General's Guidance provides increased guidance on a number of topics including but not limited to:

- the balance between the right to a fair trial and the right to private and family life (Attorney General's Office, 2020, paras 11–13);

- an illustrative guide as to how investigative material may be categorised and consequently treated (para 16);

- third party material (paras 26–58);

- digital and electronic material including the relevance of UK General Data Protection Regulation (GDPR) and the Data Protection Act to the disclosure process (paras 55–8 and Annex A);

- revelation of material to the prosecutor (paras 59–75);

- charging decision and reasonable lines of inquiry (paras 76 and 77);

- the defence case statement (paras 123–8).

COMPLEXITIES ASSOCIATED WITH DISCLOSURE

An underlying difficulty with the disclosure regime in an adversarial system (see Chapter 7 on the criminal justice system) arises because the process falls at the intersection between the investigative and trial phases. There are tensions between the objectives of each phase and the processes used to attain these objectives.

Investigations should, if conducted properly, focus on the search for an offence and an offender. The process is sensitive rather than specific – similar to a series of tests to diagnose an illness from symptoms presented.

During the investigation, there is an implicit acceptance of the inequality between the state (prosecution) and the individuals. As such, the principal trial objective is a more focused inquiry into a single closed question: is the accused guilty of the offence charged? The trial process is specific rather than sensitive. Consequently, the trial process is a more formalised one and benefits from being open and public. Unlike the investigation, the trial process must ensure equality and respect for due process. The neutrality of the process is reflected in the prosecutor's role as a minister of justice.

SUMMARY OF KEY CONCEPTS

This chapter has explored disclosure and covered some of the following key concepts.

How and why there are rules about disclosure.

How disclosure fits into the adversarial system of justice.

The legal requirements for disclosure and the impact of not getting it right.

Individual and agencies' responsibility for disclosure.

Key terminology within disclosure.

The meaning and approach with various 'categories' of material.

Some of the complexities associated with disclosure.

CHECK YOUR KNOWLEDGE

1. What is the legislation that underpins disclosure?

2. Which legislation states that individuals have the right to a fair trial?

3. Investigations only need to focus on finding the evidence to convict the person responsible – true/false?

4. What are the three types of investigation?

5. Under what section of what Act is material defined?

6. You only have to disclose information that supports the prosecution case – true/false?

7. Once you have completed disclosure once, there is no need to consider it again – true/false?

Sample answers are provided at the end of this book.

FURTHER READING

BOOKS

Cook, T, Hill, M and Hibbitt, S (2016) *Blackstone's Crime Investigators' Handbook.* Oxford: Oxford University Press.
This book provides information about the investigation of crime and the importance of disclosure.

Joyce, P (2017) Criminal Justice: An Introduction, 3rd edition. Abingdon: Routledge.
This book provides a clear introduction to the workings of the criminal justice system.

Stainton, I and Ewin, R (2022) *Criminal Investigation.* St Albans: Critical Publishing Ltd.
This book provides the reader with a guide into investigation of crime and the importance of disclosure.

JOURNAL ARTICLES

Anderson, P, Sampson, D and Gilroy, S (2021) Digital Investigations: Relevance and Confidence in Disclosure. *ERA Forum*, 22: 587–99.
This paper discusses disclosure in investigations.

Krahenbuhl, S J and Dent, H R (2021) The Views of Ex-Police Officers on Child Abuse Case Attrition in the United Kingdom. *Journal of Interpersonal Violence*, 36(3–4): 1909–32.
This paper researched the opinions of police officers' attrition in child abuse cases.

Ruyters, M, Stratton, G and Bartle, J (2021) The Culture of Non-Disclosure and Miscarriages of Justice. *Alternative Law Journal*, 46(4): 299–306.
This paper discusses the links between non-disclosure and miscarriages of justice.

WEBSITES

Attorney General's Office (2022) [online] Available at: www.gov.uk/government/organisati ons/attorney-generals-office (accessed 6 Octoboer 2022).
This website discusses the procedure of disclosure.

College of Policing (2022) Prosecution and Case Management Reference Material. [online] Available at: www.college.police.uk/app/prosecution-and-case-management/ prosecution-and-case-management-reference-material (accessed 15 November 2022).
This site gives officers guidance relating to disclosure.

Crown Prosecution Service (2022) [online] Available at: www.cps.gov.uk (accessed 6 October 2022).
The website gives guidance on disclosure.

Home Office (2020) *Manual of Guidance and MG Forms, Version 11*. [online] Available at: https://assets.publishing.service.gov.uk/government/uploads/system/uploads/ attachment_data/file/891370/Manual-of-guidance-MG-forms-v11ext.pdf (accessed 15 November 2022).
This website provides MG forms and guidance on using them.

CHAPTER 7
THE CRIMINAL JUSTICE SYSTEM

LEARNING OBJECTIVES

AFTER READING THIS CHAPTER YOU WILL BE ABLE TO:

- broadly understand the criminal justice system and models of criminal justice;

- describe the criminal court system;

- identify how offences are classified;

- understand the process of 'sending for trial';

- explain what is meant by an adversarial system;

- discuss plea and case management hearings;

- describe plea bargaining;

- understand the key components of a trial and the trial process;

- explain the purpose of bad character evidence;

- articulate some of the criticisms of the criminal justice system.

INTRODUCTION

Throughout this book you have been provided with a greater understanding of the criminal justice system and its component parts. Understanding the origins and process of criminal justice and the mechanisms that make it work is also important. It provides you with an opportunity to see how and why certain actions are undertaken to ensure a fair trial. The criminal justice system in the UK is underpinned by the concept of a fair trial, which is enshrined in the Human Rights Act 1998 Article 6 and is the cornerstone for justice in the UK.

The basis of Article 6 is that:

- *Everyone is entitled to a fair and public hearing within a reasonable time by an independent and impartial tribunal established by law. Judgment shall be pronounced publicly but the press and public may be excluded from all or part of the trial in the interest of morals, public order or national security in a democratic society, where the interests of juveniles or the protection of the private life of the parties so require, or to the extent strictly necessary in the opinion of the court in special circumstances where publicity would prejudice the interests of justice.*

- *Everyone charged with a criminal offence shall be presumed innocent until proved guilty according to law.*

- *Everyone charged with a criminal offence has the following minimum rights:*
  - *to be informed promptly, in a language which he understands and in detail, of the nature and cause of the accusation against him*
  - *to have adequate time and facilities for the preparation of his defence*
  - *to defend himself in person or through legal assistance of his own choosing or, if he has not sufficient means to pay for legal assistance, to be given it free when the interests of justice so require*
  - *to examine or have examined witnesses against him and to obtain the attendance and examination of witnesses on his behalf under the same conditions as witnesses against him*
  - *to have the free assistance of an interpreter if he cannot understand or speak the language used in court.*

(Human Rights Act 1998)

This chapter will explore the criminal justice system and its component parts, enabling you to have a clear understanding of the process as well as where your role fits in. It will also examine some of the challenges and how, on occasions, the criminal justice system has let certain individuals down.

Firstly, this chapter will begin with a critical thinking activity that will enable you to have a better understanding of trials being discontinued due to breaches of the Human Rights Act 1998 and how your future actions could prevent that.

CRITICAL THINKING ACTIVITY 7.1

LEVEL 4

There are many instances where trials have been discontinued or stopped. There are also many examples where subsequent appeals have overturned original findings, citing a breach of the Human Rights Act 1998 and/or the process used to secure a prosecution.

Conduct some research on the internet and find three cases that are evidence of such breaches or malpractice and consider what the similarities are.

- As an investigator what would you have done differently in the cases you have found to ensure the correct person was prosecuted? (Please note, this does not say convicted. This will be examined shortly.)

Sample answers are provided at the end of this book.

MODELS OF CRIMINAL JUSTICE SYSTEMS

Herbert Packer (1964) developed two key models of criminal justice that are as relevant today as when they were originally identified: the *due process* and *crime control* models of criminal justice.

THE DUE PROCESS MODEL

The due process model prioritises the interests of the individual suspect. In these cases, the individual is presumed innocent and should not be found guilty of an offence unless it is clearly defined and a formal decision-making process has been used. This model is based on the presumption that the criminal process sets legitimate obstacles which must be negotiated if a conviction is to be secured. In short, innocent until proven guilty and, as we will discuss later, the evidence presented is beyond all reasonable doubt.

The key elements of the due process model are that:

- there is a presumption of the innocence of the accused;

- there are long court battles and strict rules to ensure that the decision of the courts is not an error;

- appeals are allowed;

- the rights of the accused are prioritised;

- there is a focus on rehabilitation of convicted individuals rather than punishment, and a decision based upon the law as well as the individual situation of the accused;

- the effectiveness of the community in curbing criminal actions.

The Police and Criminal Evidence Act (PACE) 1984 was brought in following recommendations set out by the Royal Commission on Criminal Procedure. The purpose of PACE was to unify police powers under one code of practice and to carefully balance the rights of the individual against the powers of the police, in short, following the principles of the due process model.

POLICING SPOTLIGHT

On 19 March 2011, Sian O'Callaghan left a Swindon nightclub and walked to her flat 800 metres away. She never arrived at the flat and was reported missing. Some weeks later following extensive inquiries, a suspect was identified as being involved in her disappearance, a taxi driver, Chris Halliwell. He was arrested and Detective Superintendent Steve Fulcher interviewed Halliwell on a remote hillside without a lawyer present as he attempted to find out what had happened to Sian. Halliwell led Fulcher to the spot where he had dumped Sian's body before telling Fulcher he had killed another woman some years earlier, Becky Godden-Edwards. Halliwell then took Fulcher to a field where Becky's body was later found. Because Fulcher had not followed the rules, details of the interview were not deemed admissible in court. Halliwell was jailed for life for Sian's murder but only convicted for the murder of Becky in 2016.

Fulcher was heavily criticised by the Independent Police Complaints Commission (IPCC), now the Independent Office for Police Conduct (IOPC), for failing to follow the Police and Criminal Evidence Act (1984), particularly the rules following arrest.

During their investigation and subsequent report, the IPCC described Fulcher's actions as '*catastrophic, particularly on the prosecution of Mr. Halliwell for the murder of Rebecca*' and that '*[t]he Police and Criminal Evidence Act (1984) and its codes of practice are not optional. They are a fundamental part of the criminal justice process and exist to ensure the rights of suspects, and therefore the integrity of the whole process, are protected*' (IPCC, 2016, p 14).

THE CRIME CONTROL MODEL

The crime control model has been likened to an assembly line rather than an obstacle course. Its origins stem from the belief that the criminal justice system should prevent and control the committing of crimes. The intention is that it focuses on protecting society from criminals and criminal actions by regulating criminal conduct and justice. The theory is that by punishing those who commit or who are suspected of committing crimes, the rest of society will not commit crimes as frequently.

The key elements of the crime control model are that:

- there is a belief that individuals are naturally deviant and must be kept under strict control;

- there is swift and strict punishment for crimes;

- trials are conducted quickly;

- any arrest or charges of an accused imply they are guilty;

- the effectiveness of the criminal justice system is a direct means of controlling criminal activity;

- there is a decrease in the importance of individual rights, especially of criminal rights;

- the criminal justice system process should be routine and consistent, from fact finding, to trial, to sentencing, to punishment.

The following critical thinking activity explores the models and provides you with an opportunity to consider both within the example provided.

CRITICAL THINKING ACTIVITY 7.2

Imagine that you are called to a report of burglary, and when you arrive you see a person climbing out of a downstairs window, carrying a box of jewellery. Now consider the following scenarios in relation to the crime control model and the due process model.

SCENARIO 1

Under the crime control model, the police should not have to worry too much about how evidence gets collected and expanded. Investigative, arrest and search powers would be considered necessary. A crime control model would see this as a 'done deal' and that there is no need to waste time or money by ensuring individual rights and due process. Effective use of time would be to immediately punish, especially since the person was caught at the scene. Any risk of violating individual liberties would be considered secondary over the need to protect and ensure the safety of the community. Additionally, the criminal justice system is responsible for ensuring victims' rights, especially helping provide justice for those burgled.

SCENARIO 2

The due process model focuses on having a just and fair criminal justice system for all and a system that does not infringe upon individual rights. Further, this model would argue that the system should protect the rights of the individual and ensure the prosecuting authorities have followed the rules and regulations surrounding a prosecution. These involve securing the evidence, giving opportunity to explain, forensic examination and ensuring that correct disclosure and any searches under the Police and Criminal Evidence Act 1984 are fully complied with.

QUESTIONS

a) Consider the benefits and disadvantages of each each scenario.

b) Now think about a different scenario involving a suspected paedophile. Would this change your thinking as they are only suspected – what about the role of evidence?

c) Why is this now different (if it is) and how can you reconcile this across many different types of crime?

Sample answers are provided at the end of this book.

THE CRIMINAL COURT SYSTEM

Figure 7.1 provides an explanation of the UK court system, including the criminal and civil court structure. This allows you to understand how the court system and structure operates and how individuals progress through the criminal justice process.

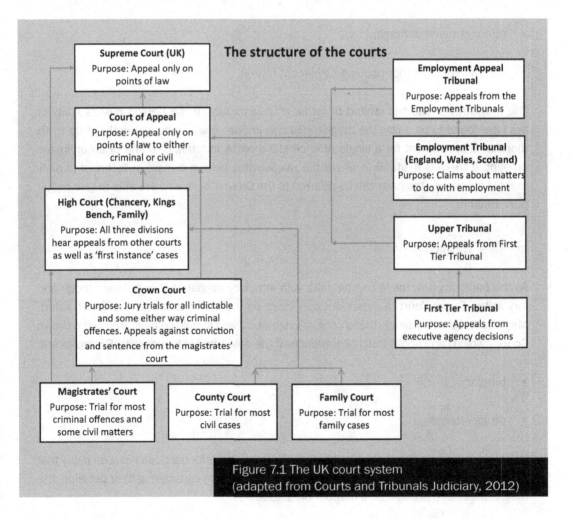

Figure 7.1 The UK court system
(adapted from Courts and Tribunals Judiciary, 2012)

CLASSIFICATION OF OFFENCES

The starting point for any criminal prosecution is usually the magistrates' court and around 95 per cent of cases will be completed there. The more serious offences are passed on to the Crown Court, either for sentencing after the defendant has been found guilty in a magistrates' court or for full trial with a judge and jury.

There are three types of offences: summary only, triable either-way and indictable only.

SUMMARY ONLY

These are less serious cases, where the defendant is not usually entitled to trial by jury. They are generally disposed of in magistrates' courts. Examples are:

- most motoring offences;

- minor criminal damage;

- common assault (not causing significant injury).

The magistrates' court is limited in terms of punishment. If the person pleads guilty or are later found to be guilty, the magistrates can impose a sentence, generally of up to six months' imprisonment for a single offence (12 months in total), or a fine of an unlimited amount. If there is a situation where the magistrates believe a more substantial punishment is necessary, the case can be referred to the Crown Court, who are able to give higher punishments.

TRIABLE EITHER-WAY

As the name implies, these can be dealt with either by magistrates or before a judge and jury at the Crown Court. A defendant can insist on their right to trial in the Crown Court. Magistrates can also decide that a case is so serious that it should be dealt with in the Crown Court – which can impose tougher sentences if the defendant is found guilty. Examples are:

- burglary;

- drugs offences.

Under the rules governing triable either-way offences, the defendant can insist on a jury trial (at the Crown Court); otherwise it is up to the magistrates. In considering their decision, the magistrates need to consider a number of factors:

- seriousness of the case;

- their sentencing powers;

- since 1996, they must take into account the defendant's plea;

- in accordance with the Criminal Justice Act 2003, *Sched.3*, magistrates will be told of a defendant's prior convictions when deciding on the mode of trial.

INDICTABLE ONLY

This includes cases regarding offences such as murder, manslaughter, rape and robbery. These must be heard at a Crown Court.

If the case is indictable only, the magistrates' court will generally decide whether to grant bail, consider other legal issues such as reporting restrictions, and then pass the case on to the Crown Court.

REFLECTIVE PRACTICE 7.1

LEVEL 4

a) Research your local courts and identify the cases heard at the magistrates' and Crown Court. The court listings will provide information about the case and its progression.

b) If you have a court close to where you live, have a visit. The general public are allowed into the courts and in most cases are allowed into the court rooms to observe. If you are able to, visit the magistrates' and the Crown Court to experience the differences.

Sample answers are provided at the end of this book.

SENDING FOR TRIAL

As we now know, all criminal trials commence in the magistrates' court, but some will go up to the Crown Court for trial or sentencing. Offences will be tried in the Crown Court if they are:

- indictable only;

- triable either-way and the mode of trial hearing in the magistrates' court results in the decision that the case should be tried in the Crown Court;

- triable either-way and the defendant chooses trial by jury in the Crown Court.

If this is the situation, cases will be transferred from the magistrates' court to the Crown Court, under one of four procedures.

1. They can be **allocated** – this is where the outcome would clearly be a higher sentence than what the magistrates can pass; or because of reasons of unusual legal, procedural or factual complexity.

2. They can be **sent** under section 51 of the Crime and Disorder Act 1998 (currently available for indictable-only offences). Section 51 (and Sch 3) states that where an adult appears or is brought before the magistrates' court charged with an offence triable only on indictment, the court will send them straight to the Crown Court for trial:

   - for that offence;

   - for any either-way or summary offence with which they are charged, which fulfils the requisite condition requisite condition.

   In addition, under section 51 the magistrates may send to the Crown Court:

   - a defendant who has already been sent to the Crown Court in respect of an indictable-only matter and who is subsequently charged with a related either-way offence;

   - adult co-defendants charged with a related triable either-way offence but who appear subsequent to a defendant already sent to the Crown Court;

   - juveniles jointly charged with a related triable either-way offence but who appear subsequent to a defendant already sent to the Crown Court;

   - juveniles sent to the Crown Court by reason of the above in respect of any related either-way or summary-only offence.

3. In certain circumstances, a case may be quickly passed to the Crown Court by way of a **notice of transfer**. Under section 4(1) of the Criminal Justice Act 1988, the prosecution may simply serve a notice on the defendant, transferring the case to the Crown Court in the case of serious fraud cases and child witness cases.

4. The prosecution may, in certain circumstances, obtain a **voluntary bill of indictment** from a High Court judge. It is a procedure to bring a case to the Crown Court

in circumstances where, for instance, the Crown believe the magistrates have wrongly decided to try the case in the magistrates' court, or whether there are other good reasons to depart from the normal process.

In transferring cases, they are sent to the most convenient Crown Court, ie convenient to parties and witnesses, thus expediting the trial. This usually means the Crown Court closest to the magistrates' court where the defendant first appears.

The Crown Court has the power to alter the place of trial and can take into account wider considerations than the magistrates in selecting a suitable location, for instance, possible prejudice to the accused if the charges have given rise to public hostility in the local area.

REFLECTIVE PRACTICE 7.2

LEVEL 4

- Consider cases that are reported on in your local press and consider them against the guidelines for allocation available on the Sentencing Council website.

- Consider the cases you have found and identify the key features that have been considered for the case allocation.

Sample answers are provided at the end of this book.

THE ADVERSARIAL SYSTEM VERSUS THE INQUISITORIAL SYSTEM

The adversarial system is based on a contest between the accused and the accuser (the victim and the state). The state (prosecution) has to draw together sufficient evidence to prove beyond reasonable doubt that the accused is guilty. This system is often referred to as a contest and is not primarily designed to establish the truth (Case et al, 2017).

In the adversarial system, the search for the truth occurs earlier during the investigation. The evidence obtained during the investigation is then tested in the court, and the prosecution has to convince a magistrate or a jury beyond all reasonable doubt that the person they are accusing is guilty. It is important to note that the accused does not have to prove that they are innocent; they merely need to raise sufficient doubt on the prosecution evidence.

The inquisitorial system is characterised by extensive pre-trial investigation and interrogations with the objective to avoid bringing an innocent person to trial. The inquisitorial process can be described as an official inquiry to ascertain the truth. The inquisitorial process grants more power to the judge who oversees the process, whereas the judge in the adversarial system serves more as an arbiter between claims of the prosecution and defence (Reichel, 2017).

Comparisons between adversarial and inquisitorial systems are shown in Table 7.1.

Table 7.1 Comparison between the adversarial and inquisitorial system

Adversarial system	Inquisitorial system
Truth through competition between the prosecution and the defence.	Truth through extensive investigation and examination of all evidence.
All parties determine what witnesses they call and the nature of the evidence they give.	The trial judge determines what witnesses to call and the order in which they are to be heard.
Previous decisions by higher courts are binding on lower courts.	Judges are free to decide each case independently of previous decisions by applying the relevant statutes.
Lawyers are active.	Lawyers are passive.
The judges pronounce judgment depending on the hearing, evidence or on the basis of examination and cross-examination.	The judge plays an active rule in questioning and hearing the parties directly.
The judges are merely passive in nature.	The judges are very active.
Case management depends upon the lawyers of both the parties.	Case management depends upon the judges.
The hearing, evidence or examination and cross-examination done by the lawyer get priority.	Documents and information about the real facts get priority.
Judges cannot exchange views with the parties for taking any decision. So, no initiative can be taken for speedy disposal of any case.	Judges sit with the parties and can exchange views for taking any decision for speedy disposal of any case.
Judges have limited discretionary power.	Judges have wide discretionary power.
Hearings can take a long time.	Reduces the time for disposing a case and to ensure speedy justice.

Now consider the two systems in relation to a real-world case in Critical Thinking Activity 7.3.

CRITICAL THINKING ACTIVITY 7.3

LEVEL 5

Consider the murder of Meredith Kercher in Perugia, Italy and the failings of the case. In 2015, when the convictions of Amanda Knox and Raffaele Sollecito were annulled, the verdict said that as scientific evidence was '*central*' to the case, there were '*sensational investigative failures*', '*amnesia*', and '*culpable omissions*' on the part of the investigating authorities.

• How could this case have been different if the investigation had taken place under an adversarial process?

Sample answers are provided at the end of this book.

PLEA AND CASE MANAGEMENT HEARINGS

The Criminal Procedure Rules 2005 introduced plea and case management (PCM) hearings, and they have been subsequently amended in 2020 (Criminal Procedure Rules 2020).

The original aim was to encourage early preparation of cases and reduce 'cracked trials', that is, a trial that has been listed for a not guilty hearing on a particular day but does not proceed, either because the defendant pleads guilty to the whole or part of the indictment, or an alternative charge, or because the prosecution offer no evidence.

The PCM hearing is the first hearing after committal to the Crown Court and is intended to ensure that the correct plea and trial process is followed. During the hearing, the judge will decide if enough information has been provided to allow a trial date to be set. At the hearing, if the defendant pleads guilty, they may be sentenced immediately, or alternatively an adjournment may be requested to allow pre-sentence reports to be completed.

If the defendant pleads guilty to some counts and not guilty to others, sentencing will be adjourned. If the defendant pleads not guilty to all counts, the prosecution and defence will inform the court of relevant details such as:

• how many witnesses they intend to call;

• any evidence they intend to exhibit.

The court will then be given an estimate of how long the trial is likely to run for, along-side when witnesses will be likely to have to attend court. The judge will ensure sufficient directions are put into place to allow the trial to proceed as soon as possible.

PLEA BARGAINING

Plea bargaining is a process whereby the offender agrees to plead guilty to a lesser charge, thus dispensing with the need to go through the whole trial process to prove their guilt. It is common practice for the defence to seek to minimise the impact of a criminal charge against their client by offering a guilty plea to a lesser offence.

Plea bargaining most often occurs in the following scenarios:

- where a defendant testifies against a co-conspirator;

- where a lesser charge is offered due to the difficulty of proving the greater charge.

It is a matter for the defendant to decide whether to offer a guilty plea to a lesser offence and for the prosecution to decide whether to accept it. In *R v Goodyear* (2005) it was ruled that a defendant can request an indication from the judge as to the likely sentence if they plead guilty.

The prosecution should only do so where they consider that the evidence will not realistic-ally support a conviction for the more serious offence, or where the public interest other-wise justifies accepting a plea to a lesser charge. The Code for Crown Prosecutors states that prosecutors should only accept the defendant's plea if they think the court is able to pass a sentence that matches the seriousness of the offending, particularly where there are aggravating features. Prosecutors must never accept a guilty plea just because it is convenient.

For these reasons, plea bargaining is really a process of negotiation in which the defence set out the weaknesses in the evidence with a view to persuading the prosecution to change its view of the case. The benefit to the defendant can be the offer of a lesser charge and the benefit to the prosecution the avoidance of a trial which can be costly, time-consuming and may require witnesses to attend court and potentially relive trau-matic events.

Plea bargaining negotiations have to be carried out carefully and sensitively. Victims of crime do not want to find out at the last moment that a 'deal' has been carried out behind their backs and a guilty plea has been accepted to an offence which does not begin to reflect the seriousness of what has happened to them. For this reason, the Farquharson Guidelines impose a duty on prosecution advocates to consult where possible with victims or their families before accepting a plea to an alternative offence.

REFLECTIVE PRACTICE 7.3

LEVEL 4

Consider the following scenario:

> A person is charged with causing grievous bodily harm with intent (Offences Against the Person Act 1861, s.18), which carries a maximum term of life imprisonment. The lesser offence of inflicting grievous bodily harm (Offences Against the Person Act 1861, s.20) carries a maximum term of five years' imprisonment. We are aware that imposing maximum terms is very rare, but in real terms, the sentence for a section 18 offence will be significantly longer than the sentence for a section 20 offence. For this reason, if the defendant consents, the defence will often offer a guilty plea to a section 20 offence in place of a section 18.

- If you were the prosecutor what would you consider, and what would be the main points that would sway your decision?

Sample answers are provided at the end of this book.

KEY COMPONENTS OF A TRIAL

The burden of proof at a trial is for the prosecution. They need to show beyond all reasonable doubt that the defendant is guilty. By comparison, the defendant only needs to introduce an element of doubt and the magistrates or the jury at Crown Court must find the defendant not guilty.

This section will explore the trial process (see Figure 7.2) and links to the court structure shown in Figure 7.1.

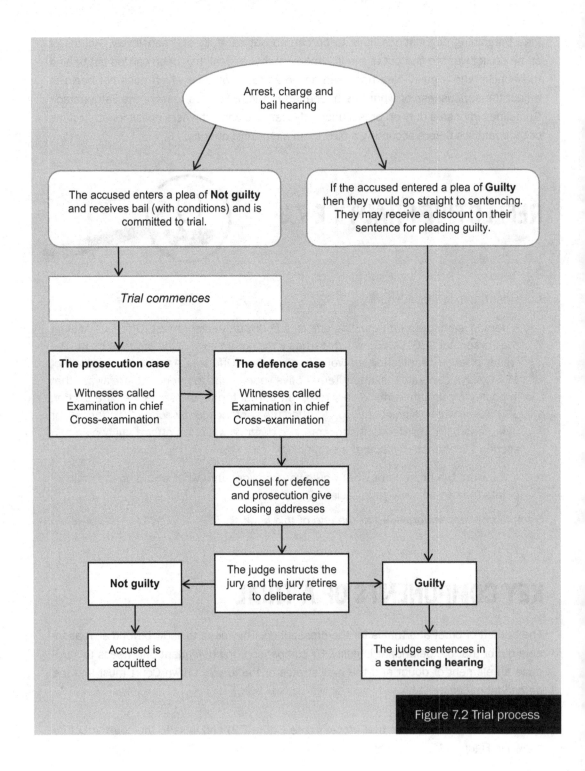

Figure 7.2 Trial process

BAD CHARACTER EVIDENCE

Bad character is when the defendant has previous convictions for offences similar to those they are on trial for. The prosecution may want to rely on bad character evidence of the accused to show their character and propensity to criminal behaviour. Conversely, the defence may want to use the bad character of a witness to show they should not be trusted to tell the truth.

Bad character is defined in the Criminal Justice Act 2003 as follows:

> *s.98 Bad character*
>
> *References... to evidence of a person's 'bad character' are to evidence of, or of a disposition towards, misconduct on his part, other than evidence which—*
>
> *(a) has to do with the alleged facts of the offence with which the defendant is charged, or*
>
> *(b) is evidence of misconduct in connection with the investigation or prosecution of that offence.*
>
> *s.112 Interpretation*
>
> *'misconduct' means the commission of an offence or other reprehensible behaviour;*
>
> (Criminal Justice Act 2003, sections 98 and 112)

Bad character includes evidence of:

- convictions or cautions, and/or;

- other 'reprehensible' behaviour, and;

- which in either case do not specifically relate to the facts of the offence being tried at court, or to the investigation or prosecution of that offence.

'Reprehensible behaviour' is not specifically defined in the Criminal Justice Act 2003. What could be considered reprehensible in one set of circumstances might not be so considered in another; each case is different and must be viewed on its own facts.

Where it is intended to rely on bad character evidence, a bad character application must be made to the court, ie to the judge (in the Crown Court) or the magistrates or district judge (in the magistrates' court), who will rule on whether the evidence can be used at trial.

The only exception to this is where the prosecution and all defendants in the trial agree to the evidence being admitted, in which case the court should be informed of this and the purposes for which the evidence will be used at trial.

The evidence-based policing feature below shows an interesting example of using bad character evidence.

EVIDENCE-BASED POLICING

In the case of *R v Hanson* [2005], the defendant pleaded guilty to theft and was sentenced to nine months' detention. The prosecution introduced the evidence of the defendant's previous convictions for dishonesty. The prosecution argued that this evidence was important in determining whether the defendant had a propensity to commit offences of this kind.

The defendant argued that his previous convictions for dishonesty did not demonstrate a propensity to commit burglary.

CRITICISMS OF THE CRIMINAL JUSTICE SYSTEM

As with many systems and processes, there will be criticisms and individuals who provide critique. In the UK, many criticisms are based on the processes within the criminal justice system. Within this chapter we have discussed some, for example cracked and ineffective trials within the context of plea and case management. This section will explore some of the key criticisms.

DISCLOSURE

Other areas discussed in previous chapters include the impact that disclosure under the Criminal Procedure and Investigations Act 1996 has on trials. The failure to disclose evidence in accordance with the legal requirements has significant impact. The Crown Prosecution Service have reported that in the first six months of 2021, over 1600 cases collapsed.

POLICING SPOTLIGHT

Liam Allan was wrongly accused of 12 counts of rape and sexual assault in 2017. The criminology student was cleared after it emerged that police had failed to disclose phone texts that undermined their case. Mr Allan was charged with multiple allegations of rape and sexual assault. He was arrested and spent two years on bail before the start of his Crown Court trial. The prosecution case concluded, on the basis of the complainant's evidence, that Mr Allan had assaulted and raped her. She said she did not consent to sex with Mr Allan and that she did not enjoy sex and would not have consented to sex.

Part way through the trial, the complainant's undisclosed telephone records were properly reviewed by the prosecution and disclosed to the judge and defence team. The text messages on the phone showed that the complainant sent a series of text messages to Mr Allan asking for more sex. In fact, she wanted violent sex and spoke about wanting to be raped. In a further round of texts, she made it clear to a friend that no crime had been committed. Mr Allan had raised the issue of text messages in his police interview, but the police say that the phone evidence was not properly considered. The officer in the case ignored clear guidelines on disclosure – which require them to disclose all relevant material in a case.

CONFESSION EVIDENCE AND MISCARRIAGES OF JUSTICE

Where the admissibility of confession evidence is challenged under section 76 of PACE, the prosecution must establish beyond reasonable doubt that the confession was not in fact made as a result of oppression, nor in circumstances which were likely to have made it unreliable.

The term 'oppression' for the purposes of section 76 of PACE includes *'torture, inhuman or degrading treatment, and the use or threat of violence'*. This reflects the wording of Article 3 of the European Convention on Human Rights. The meaning of the term was also considered by the Court of Appeal in the case of *R v Fulling* [1987] 2 All ER 65. The court held that 'oppression' was to be given its ordinary dictionary meaning and was likely to involve some impropriety on the part of the interrogator (CPS, 2022).

UNRELIABLE CONFESSIONS

Unreliable confessions were given a broad interpretation by the Court of Appeal in *R v Fulling* (see above). This included:

- confessions obtained as the result of an inducement – for example, a promise of bail or a promise that a prosecution would not arise from the confession;

- hostile and aggressive questioning;

- failure to record accurately what was said;

- failure to caution;

- failure to provide an appropriate adult where one is required;

- failure to comply with the Code of Practice in relation to the detention of the accused – for example, a failure to allow sufficient rest prior to an interview;

- failure of the defence solicitor or appropriate adult to act properly – for example, by making interjections during the interview which are hostile to the defendant. It is important that prosecutors take into consideration whether confessions can be adduced to be reliable or not by the courts.

ROLE OF EXPERT WITNESSES

Experts can be of great assistance within the court process to understand the issues in a case, including the guilt or innocence of the accused. Prosecutors require an appropriate knowledge and understanding of the evidence in question to present and challenge expert evidence.

An expert witness can provide the court with a statement of opinion on any admissible matter calling for expertise by the witness if they are qualified to give such an opinion. The duty of an expert witness is to help the court to achieve the overriding objective by giving an opinion which is objective and unbiased, in relation to matters within their expertise.

The following policing spotlight highlights a significant case where expert evidence was eventually challenged and found to be misleading.

POLICING SPOTLIGHT

In 1999, Sally Clark, a solicitor, was convicted at Chester Crown Court of murdering her two infant sons (one in 1996 and the other in 1998). Her defence had argued that the children had died of Sudden Infant Death Syndrome (SIDS), but expert witness, Professor Sir Roy Meadow, told the court that the probability of two children from an affluent family suffering SIDS was 1 in 73 million. She unsuccessfully appealed against her conviction in 2000. Her solicitor, Marilyn Stowe, had concerns about the statistical basis of Professor Meadow's evidence which had led to Sally Clark being sentenced to life in prison.

An independent pathologist reviewed the medical notes of both infants and discovered that one of the babies had in fact died from a viral infection, not cot death. This evidence was not presented at the initial trial. The appeal was successful, and the conviction was quashed. This case raised important questions about the reliability of expert evidence.

Always consider the expertise of the expert and how their claims are justified. Think about their evidence as you would any other piece of evidence and apply a critical and investigative mindset.

TREATMENT OF VICTIMS AND WITNESSES

Some victims, including those of the most serious sexual offences such as rape, are at risk of coming face to face with defendants because courts are not set up to deliver the protections the law provides for them while giving evidence (Baird, 2021).

The court system allows witnesses to be questioned but considering the impact this has on witnesses during some cases identifies challenges. Sometimes the witness will not give evidence or will become upset, to the extent that they cannot provide their evidence. This could potentially lead to the prosecution failing.

To aide witnesses to give their evidence, 'special measures' are a series of provisions to help vulnerable and intimidated witnesses to give their best evidence in court and help to relieve some of the stress and anxiety associated with giving evidence. These measures can include:

- screens to shield them from the defendant;

- giving their evidence by television link either from a separate room at the court building or using remote evidence centres;

- allowing evidence to be pre-recorded;

- using trained communications specialists to help witnesses while giving evidence.

However, recent findings from the Victims' Commissioner, Dame Vera Baird KC, have suggested that victims and witnesses are falling through the gaps and not being offered appropriate special measures (Baird, 2021).

It is important, therefore, that you make sure that you consider the needs of the witness to ensure they are able to give the best evidence without being intimidated by the court system.

ROLE OF THE MEDIA – CONTEMPT OF COURT

As the impact of the media and in particular social media becomes more apparent in society, we can see the influence it has on cases in courts. Mainstream media are controlled through guidance and legislation; however, the emergence of social media raises other challenges. The Attorney General's Office provide some examples of individuals breaching the rules and acting in contempt of court.

- In July 2015, two teenage girls were put on trial for the murder of Angela Wrightson. Due to the age of the defendants, they were granted anonymity and referred to by their initials (D & F). After only two days, the judge suspended the trial after hundreds of posts purporting to reveal the identities of the two girls appeared on social media. Aborting the trial cost the public tens of thousands of pounds and led to justice being delayed. Both defendants were subsequently jailed for a minimum of 15 years in April 2016 following a reconstituted trial at Leeds Crown Court.

- In January 2018, in the trial of two of KM's [a defendant] relatives, the court issued an order imposing reporting restrictions on naming or identifying two witnesses in the proceedings. Despite the court order, KM posted videos and photos that she had taken in the courtroom during the trial that identified the two prosecution witnesses on Facebook. The posts also alleged the witnesses were lying and encouraged others to share the post and tag the witnesses. KM was later found in contempt of court and given a 12-week prison sentence, suspended for two years and ordered to pay £2000 in costs.

- In August 2019, despite signs warning against recording the proceedings, EH [the defendant] streamed more than an hour's footage from her partner's Crown Court trial to Facebook. This footage was downloaded hundreds of times. At her High Court hearing in October 2020, EH apologised for her actions, claiming that she was unaware of the laws around recording court proceedings. However, the court found that she had been warned against recording the trial the week before it started. In February 2021, she was sentenced to a four-month prison term, suspended for two years, and ordered to pay £500 in costs, after being found in contempt of court.

These examples show what actions can be considered as contempt of court and the impact of those actions on those who have breached them.

CONCLUSION

This chapter has provided you with an overview of the criminal justice system, the models of criminal justice and how they operate in the UK. It has explained how offences are classified and how a defendant would pass through the system at the various stages, including consideration of the impact of the severity of the crime. This chapter has explored the differences between an adversarial and an inquisitorial system, and what this means in terms of investigation and outcomes. You should understand the trial process and some of the key evidential factors, including bad character evidence; this also links to disclosure that we discussed in Chapter 6, so you should now be able to see how everything is interlinked. Finally, the chapter has considered some of the criticisms of the criminal justice system and how this impacts on trials and outcomes at court.

SUMMARY OF KEY CONCEPTS

This chapter has explored the criminal justice system and covered some of the following key concepts.

⚙ **The foundations and principles of the criminal justice system, based on Article 6 of the European Convention on Human Rights.**

⚙ **The process and stages associated with the court processes and an understanding of the complexities of the system.**

⚙ **Some of the key components of a trial and transition between courts.**

⚙ **Key issues to consider when gathering and presenting evidence.**

⚙ **Some of the criticisms of the criminal justice system, connected to the court and trial process.**

CHECK YOUR KNOWLEDGE

1. How does Article 6 of the European Convention on Human Rights impact on the UK criminal justice system?

2. What is a summary-only offence and in which court can it be heard?

3. What are the differences between Packer's models of criminal justice?

4. Why do we have plea bargaining in the UK court system?

⟶

5. What is the impact of unreliable confession?

6. Are expert witnesses helpful in a prosecution and why?

Sample answers are provided at the end of this book.

FURTHER READING

BOOKS

Case, S, Johnson, P, Manlow, D, Smith, R, Williams, K, Samota, N and Ugwudike, P (2017) *Criminology*. New York: Oxford University Press.
This is a comprehensive book that examines the causes and impacts of crime and the key issues we have touched on in this chapter.

Davies, M, Croall, H and Tyrer, J (1999) *Criminal Justice*. London: Longman.
This is a good book that explains the criminal justice system.

JOURNAL ARTICLES

Crous, C (2011) Managing Covert Human Intelligence Sources: Lessons for Police Commanders. *Australasian Policing*, 3(2): 12–15.
This article offers insights into the handling of covert human intelligence sources (CHIS), constant training required and reviews examples from the UK, and Northern Ireland, plus data over six months from Australia.

WEBSITES

Courts and Tribunals Judiciary (2022) [online] Available at: www.judiciary.uk (accessed 6 October 2022).
The website discusses the criminal justice system.

Crown Prosecution Service (2022) [online] Available at: www.cps.gov.uk (accessed 6 October 2022).
The website discusses the criminal justice system.

CHAPTER 8
REHABILITATION, ONSET OFFENDING AND DISTRACTION TECHNIQUES

LEARNING OBJECTIVES

AFTER READING THIS CHAPTER YOU WILL BE ABLE TO:

⚙ **explain the importance of working to reduce victimisation;**

⚙ **understand distraction techniques;**

⚙ **comprehend the issue of onset offending.**

INTRODUCTION

Throughout this book you have discovered the powers and processes that as a police officer you must understand when dealing with those that are suspected of committing crime. However, the 'nine pillars of policing', introduced by Sir Robert Peel in 1829, have at their heart the requirement for police officers to reduce or prevent crime. This chapter is dedicated to the need for you, as a modern-day police officer, to understand the mechanics of practices that can be put in place to prevent crime when dealing with those that have the potential to commit crime.

It is important to understand when and why a person first commits an offence. This is commonly referred to as 'onset offending' which, it has been argued, is up to three to five years prior to the person's first interaction with the criminal justice service. Onset offending will be discussed to allow you to have a full understanding of the reasoning behind such a theory. This links to the need to move persons away from the possibility of offending by working with your partners, as discussed within the Crime and Disorder Act 1998, to distract offenders from crime at an early age.

By developing this knowledge in the daily workings of policing, it has the potential to reduce the numbers of people that are victimised by crime. While various academics discuss the need to ensure that crime prevention and the ten principles of crime prevention also assist with reducing victimisation, others argue that more effort should be given to assist and move potential offenders away from a life of crime. The College of Policing website is a useful tool to refer to when discussing the prevention of crime and the prevention of persons becoming offenders.

Throughout this chapter the following policing spotlight scenario will be utilised so you can consider options to assist in a community issue and reduce the potential of the actors becoming involved in crime.

POLICING SPOTLIGHT

You are the local community police officer for the area of Wanbourne; it is a built-up area with a large residential area which also contains a small industrial area to the west. There are two schools: a primary school (St Wanbourne) and a high school (Little Wanbourne). The population of the area is approximately 100,000 persons with a large youth presence of approximately 8000. The unemployment rate in the area runs at 35 per cent due to the recent pandemic and the closing of a local food processing plant. The crime rates in the area are comparable with the rest of the policing area and no higher than current national trends. Within Wanbourne there is a retirement village and on the outskirts there is a large open-plan area with trees where the local youths are known to hang around. There have been allegations of underage drinking and some drug usage; there has also been some minor damage (criminal damage) to fencing around the area and littering. No arrests have been made. You have been called to the retirement village and on arrival the residents share concerns about the growing problem and tell you that they are fearful to walk in the area, especially at night.

REFLECTIVE PRACTICE 8.1

LEVEL 4

- Consider the above scenario and imagine you are in the place of the police officer. What suggestions would you make to tackle the problem at the moment?

CRITICAL THINKING ACTIVITY 8.1

LEVEL 5

- Read the scenario below and critically evaluate the following question.

    The local inspector tasks the police units to ensure that they stop and search any youth who they reasonably suspect of carrying alcohol and remove it from them.

- What effect is this likely to have on the youth in the area and can comparisons be made to the issues highlighted in the Scarman Report?

ONSET OFFENDING

Onset offending is the age at which the perpetrator first commits an offence; however, perpetrators have self-reported that the onset behaviour commenced some three to five years prior to first arrest and conviction (Theobold and Farrington, 2014). The earlier a person enters into a criminal career, the longer that career will be. We will now discuss static theory, which explains that criminal behaviour can be linked to the person's upbringing, and then hostile attribution bias, which explores why a person stops offending, attributing this to behavioural change such as a change in lifestyle.

STATIC THEORY

Static theory states that behaviours emerge in a predictable sequence and unfold at roughly the same age for all individuals. According to this theory, the causes of criminal behaviour are established early in life and are relatively stable and unaffected by events. Youths who experience poor parenting and have harsh, brittle relationships with their parents, for example, are likely to have low self-control and therefore relatively high levels of offending at all ages. According to static theory, individuals tend to maintain their general position relative to others with respect to their levels of offending. The peak of adolescent offending is assumed to be the result of normative developmental changes. Static theory assumes a plasticity to human behaviour that persists throughout life and acknowledges the importance of early individual and parenting differences, contending that changing social environments are the primary drivers of offending behaviour. According to dynamic models, continuing to offend into adulthood is the outcome of processes were set in motion by earlier developmental issues. Young offenders who stop committing crimes are those who re-establish bonds of conventional society and engage in pro-social activities.

HOSTILE ATTRIBUTION BIAS

Hostile attribution bias is a social psychological explanation for why criminal behaviour continues into adulthood; the bias is linked to attributing negative intention to others. It is recognised by academics that the first step to remove oneself from criminal behaviour is a behaviour change (Theobold and Farrington, 2014). This usually occurs when the person redefines themselves and sees that criminal behaviour is no longer compatible with their new identity or lifestyle, such as marriage and employment. Glueck (1937) argued that the only factor that emerges as significant in the reformative process was age, in terms of whether they would grow out of the criminality or they become too old to commit the offences, meaning the chances of being caught increased. Theobold and Farrington (2014) state that a child's reason for onset offending can be linked to neuropsychological problems, low intelligence and high impulsiveness combined with poverty and poor parenting. They further argue that those who first commit offences as an adult or whose onset offending is in the adult years are completely different as they tend to be persons who are nervous, withdrawn and have few friends from childhood.

Onset offending is an area of academic study that continues to develop theories of why a person first commits offences and enters a life of crime. Now consider the critical thinking activity below to further explore the theory of onset offending.

CRITICAL THINKING ACTIVITY 8.2

LEVEL 6

- Critically analyse the theory of onset offending. Does it explain all offending that takes place or is it looking for an answer where there is none?

DISTRACTION TECHNIQUES

As a police officer working within Safer Neighbourhood teams, you may be given the opportunity to work with statutory partners such as the council on projects that are designed to distract offenders away from a life of crime. In the past, such schemes or groups have been criticised by the media, for example for allowing those that stole cars to attend workshops to develop skills to be able to repair vehicles. As you have seen from the section above on onset offending, a person is likely to stop offending if there is a change in their lifestyle, such as employment or a new interest. It can therefore be argued that while some of the programmes have been criticised, there is research available to suggest that distraction works.

It is important, however, to note that very different effects are evidenced from different programmes within broadly similar approaches, and a single programme can have a different impact on different individuals. A good resource for information in respect of distraction techniques is *What Works to Reduce Reoffending: A Summary of the Evidence* (Gov.Scot, 2015).

There is an assumption that people can change or that a person's past is not their destiny. Under a moral redeemability belief system, 'criminality' is not a permanent trait of individuals, but rather an adaptation to a person's life circumstances that can be changed by altering those circumstances or self-understanding (Maruna and King, 2009). This is further evidence that there is a need to engage with persons that have committed offences or are likely to commit offences to assist them in removing themselves from criminality.

Distraction techniques or offender behaviour programmes can include the following:

- workshops – including educational programmes;

- anger management courses;

- social interaction courses;

- youth workers/activities (gyms/mechanics);

- unpaid work – working within the voluntary sector;

- time management courses.

Other programmes have also involved giving youths responsibility for an area such as a youth pod. This idea was trialled by Thames Valley Police in the early 2000s and the findings were that when the young people were involved in the project, it reduced criminality in the area of the youth pod. Similar schemes have been applied throughout the country to reduce crime.

These offender behaviour programmes and interventions aim to change the thinking, attitudes and behaviours which may lead people to reoffend. They encourage pro-social attitudes and goals for the future and are designed to help people develop new skills to stop their offending. These include:

- problem solving;

- perspective taking;

- managing relationships;

- self-management.

Offending behaviour programmes often use cognitive-behavioural techniques. There is good international evidence that such activity is effective in reducing reoffending and preventing offending (Gov.uk, 2002). Moving a potential offender towards such a distraction technique can prevent the person from becoming involved in the criminal justice system and further, for victims of crime, it will also reduce the calls to service for the police. Now consider the following reflective practice and critical thinking activities.

REFLECTIVE PRACTICE 8.2

LEVEL 5

Re-read the scenario at the start of this chapter and consider the following.

- What measures could you suggest to reduce the possibility of crime in the area of Wanbourne?

CRITICAL THINKING ACTIVITY 8.3

LEVEL 6

- Having discussed distraction techniques, critically analyse the effects of such programmes and their true effects on crime rates. If they are so successful, why are they not being used to reduce knife crime?

REDUCING VICTIMISATION

As a police officer you will need understand what a victim is, and, by understanding the theories discussed here, why a person becomes a victim. You can then help to reduce victimisation within your policing area by utilising the knowledge you have gleaned. In recent years, the victim has become more important within the criminal justice service with the need to protect victims and witnesses from the impact of crime on their lives. This includes their role within the criminal justice service such as attending court. Victimology is an area of academic study that is gaining in status and authority and victim theories will be discussed within this section. In 1985, the United Nations defined a victim as:

Persons who, collectively or individually, have suffered harm, including physical or mental injury, emotional suffering, economic loss or substantial impairment of their fundamental rights, through acts or omissions that are in violation of criminal laws operating within Member States, including those laws proscribing criminal abuse of power...

Thus, this indicates the importance placed by governing bodies in the development of a victims' charter to ensure victims were treated fairly.

Since this time, several improvements to the criminal justice service have been completed to ensure that the victim has a better experience, including:

- victims have the right to make personal or impact statements;

- dispute resolution;

- restorative justice.

The Home Office has gone further, stating '*[t]he concerns of victims of crime are at the heart of the work we do*' (Gov.uk, 2019), and demonstrating the importance that the government place on ensuring that victims of crime feel that their issues are being taken seriously.

As you will see in Table 8.1, in the 1930s Benjamin Mendelsohn created a typology of victims and tried to explain how people became victims. While this study related to victims of rape, it has been accepted as an explanation of why a person becomes a victim. However, Von Hentig's typology (see Table 8.2) develops this concept further. Even though the area of study is starting to be recognised and have a higher status in academic thinking, academics have considered why a person becomes a victim of crime for some time. The typology is therefore arguing that any victim will fit in to at least one of the categories listed but it could be argued that such a typology could lean towards victim blaming and not putting the victim first.

Table 8.1 Mendelsohn's typology of crime victims

Innocent victim	A person who is in the wrong place at the wrong time; no involvement in the incident.
	Often referred to as the perfect victim.
The victim with minor guilt	No active involvement with the victimisation but has a minor contrition factor, such as frequenting locations known for high crime or associating with criminals.
The guilty victim, guilty offender	Both may have been engaged in criminal endeavours such as car theft or drug supply.
The guilty offender, guiltier victim	Initial attack by offender, but victim wins the fight causing injury to the offender.
Guilty victim	Offender instigated offence such as domestic abuse but is killed by the victim.
Imaginary victim	Those that make false reports.

(Adapted from Mendelsohn, 1976)

Table 8.2 Von Hentig's typology

Young people	Have adult supervision such as parents or guardians, lack physical strength, lack mental and emotional maturity and due to this lack the ability to recognise victimisation.
Female/elderly	Physical strength lacking
Mentally ill/intellectually disabled	Physical strength lacking

Immigrants	Threat of deportation and lack of understanding of local customs.
Dull normal	Easily deceived due to being naïve or vulnerable.
The depressed	Not vigilant, and gullible.
The acquisitive	Targeted by scammers due to greed and wish to achieve a financial advantage.
The lonesome and broken-hearted	Susceptible to manipulation due to desire to have a partner.
Tormentors	Abusers in relationships becoming victims when the tables are turned.
Blocked, exempted and fighting victims	Likely to enter unsuitable situations where they are taken advantage of.

(adapted from Von Hentig, 1948)

A controversial and outdated theory that supports that the victim has a proportion of responsibility is the victim precipitation theory; Amir (1971) claimed that rape victims may contribute to their attacks by pursuing a relationship with the rapist. However aberrant such an explanation is of why someone becomes a victim, this is an example of academic thinking back in the 1970s.

It is further suggested that there is an 'ideal' victim that will fit into the requirements of the public's perception of what a victim should be (Durisin and van der Meulen, 2021).

Consider the below policing spotlight feature.

POLICING SPOTLIGHT

CONSIDER THESE TWO CASES.

1. Milly Dowler, a middle-class girl from a seemingly stable family background who had never previously gone missing, was splashed on the front pages of national newspapers within days as her disappearance attracted national attention, fulfilling the news media's criteria for a model middle-class schoolgirl. Milly Dowler's body was finally found in September 2002, six months after she disappeared, although it was almost a decade before the conviction of her killer Levi Bellfield in 2011.

⟶

2. Hannah Williams disappeared in April 2001. She a girl from a working-class single-parent home who had spent time in care and had a history of running away – she attracted scant coverage in the media. Her body was discovered in March 2002. A police spokesperson described Williams' mother as '*not really press conference material*' and, while Dowler continued to dominate newspaper headlines, Williams was almost immediately forgotten in the news media. The National Missing Persons Helpline noted, in commenting upon the case, that news media treating such stories would often ask for cases where the subject was female, within a particular age range and with a particular social background.

CRITICAL THINKING ACTIVITY 8.4

- The 'ideal victim' theory is highlighted above in the two cases which present strikingly different media coverage of two similar cases. Critically analyse the statements made. Can you identify factors within the cases that may lead to prejudice and the reasons why?

Other criminological theories on victims include lifestyle theory, whereby their lifestyle increases their exposure to criminal offenders, or deviant lifestyle theory, whereby the victim becomes a victim due to the lifestyle they lead such as drug use. The majority of victims can be linked with ease to routine activity theory, whereby three elements need to be present in order for a person to become a victim of crime: the availability of a suitable target (a home containing sellable items), the absence of a suitable guardian (such as a police officer) and the presence of a motivated offender (such as a drug user). Without one of these elements, a crime would not be completed. Therefore, if as a police officer you are able to remove a point in the triangle you can prevent a person being victimised by a crime.

By utilising this material in this book, you now have the knowledge and understanding of dealing with potential offenders and by considering onset offending, distraction techniques and victim theory you have the tools to remove one of the points of the triangle and reduce crime in your policing area.

REFLECTIVE PRACTICE 8.3

LEVEL 5/6

Consider the scenario at the beginning of the chapter concerning the elderly population in the retirement home and the issues they are reporting to the police. They are the victims even though they have not been subject to a crime personally. They fear crime in their area and it stops them from enjoying the surrounding area. Consider your new knowledge from reading this chapter.

- What actions can you suggest to the shift inspector to restore the public confidence in the police in this area?

- What preventative measures can you put in place?

- What distraction techniques could you suggest?

- What are you doing to consider the potential victims?

- Can you remove one of the tips of the triangle to prevent the crime?

SUMMARY OF KEY CONCEPTS

This chapter discussed onset offending, distraction techniques and victims of crime. The following key concepts were covered.

- **Onset offending is the time when a person commits their first criminal offence.**

- **Distraction techniques are used to prevent persons turning to crime.**

- **The Home Office have created a victims' charter.**

- **All victims of crime can be linked to the rational choice theory.**

CHECK YOUR KNOWLEDGE

1. Most offenders when asked about onset offending usually claim the offending commenced how many years before?

2. The Home Office have stated they have put someone at the forefront of everything they do – who is this?

3. Name five distraction techniques.

4. When was Mendelsohn's typology created?

5. Glueck (1937) stated there is only one reason persons stop committing crime – what is it?

Sample answers are provided at the end of this book.

FURTHER READING

BOOKS

Newman, T (2005) *Handbook of Policing*. Abingdon: Willan Publishing.
This book concentrates on the role of a police officer and covers the duties of a police officer.

WEBSITES

College of Policing (2022) APP (Authorised Professional Practice). [online] Available at: www.app.college.police.uk (accessed 6 October 2022).
This website provides a searchable resource covering guidance on many aspects of police powers.

College of Policing (2022) Policing Guidance [online] Available at www.college.police.uk/ guidance (accessed 6 October 2022).
The College of Policing authorised professional practice (APP) web pages provide a searchable resource, covering guidance on many aspects of police powers.

Gov.scot (2015) What Works to Reduce Reoffending: A Summary of the Evidence. [online] Available at: www.gov.scot/publications/works-reduce-reoffending-summary-evidence/ (accessed 11 October 2022).
This website provides further reading on distraction techniques.

SAMPLE ANSWERS

CHAPTER 1

CHECK YOUR KNOWLEDGE

1. Sir Robert Peel

2. 1829

3. Police and Criminal Evidence Act 1984

4. Code A

5. 176

CHAPTER 2

CHECK YOUR KNOWLEDGE

1. 1982

2. 1983

3. 1984

4. GOWISLEY

5. 19 pieces of legislation cover stop and search powers

CHAPTER 3

CHECK YOUR KNOWLEDGE

1. Four plus additional powers in PACE

2. Two

3. 24 hours

4. Section 24

5. Section 32 of PACE

CHAPTER 4

CHECK YOUR KNOWLEDGE

1. Yes

2. Nine

3. One

4. Five years

5. Legal Aid, Sentencing and Punishment of Offenders Act 2012

CHAPTER 5

CHECK YOUR KNOWLEDGE

1. Five

2. Open

3. Room availability, equipment, legal representative, appropriate adult, interpreter

4. 1992

5. Birmingham Six and Guildford Four

CHAPTER 6

REFLECTIVE PRACTICE 6.1

a) The victims can be left traumatised by their experience this can have long-lasting effects on their well being their lives and their wider associations.

b) The suspect may feel they have got away with a crime they have committed and go on to continue to target the victim or commit further offences within the community.

c) The effects to the criminal justice system can be that the community no longer has confidence in the procedures of the courts and, as the police are seen as the front line of the criminal justice system, they can be seen as unable to complete their role.

d) This can lead to wide reaching effects on the community which can range from distrust of the police to vigilante behaviour by the community to protect their property.

CRITICAL THINKING ACTIVITY 6.1

The statement is correct: there is no need for a case to collapse if all parties have followed the guidance of rules of disclosure. We can see in this chapter that disclosure is complex but vitally important to any case. Consider a simple shoplifting case and what you would need to disclose. Now consider a headline case in the news following a murder or serious incident, how would you start to think about disclosure?

CRITICAL THINKING ACTIVITY 6.2

Within this scenario you are not told which computers have been used for accessing the material and you must prove your case beyond all reasonable doubt. So seizure of all computers could be argued as reasonable; however, it would be for the investigating officer to justify the reasons. As shown here the case you have looked at is becoming more commonplace in UK policing and will only get more complex. Think about the number of electronic devices you have linked to the internet that you can message from, computers, phones, watches, games consoles, to name a few. Critical decision making is a key part of policing – what are you going to seize and why? More importantly, what are you *not* going to seize and why as any defence will question you about this. Remember, the prosecution has to prove their case 'beyond all reasonable doubt'.

CRITICAL THINKING ACTIVITY 6.3

In the previous two activities, you have considered the challenges of disclosure. Think about the implications of disclosing everything you have linked to a case. In other books in this series, you will read about some sensitive policing tactics that should not be disclosed. What about other forms of sensitive material, medical records or other confidential documentation? What would be the impact in the future if you knew everything about you could be disclosed; would you give the information in the first instance?

CHECK YOUR KNOWLEDGE

1. Criminal Procedure and Investigations Act 1996 (CPIA 1996).

2. Article 6 of the European Convention on Human Rights.

3. False, the investigator should pursue all reasonable lines of inquiry, whether these point towards or away from the suspect and may extend to material in the hands of a third party.

4. Investigations into crimes that have been committed; investigations to ascertain whether a crime has been committed; and investigations which begin in the belief that a crime may be committed.

5. Section 23(1) of the Criminal Procedure and Investigations Act 1996.

6. False – all unused material should be disclosed.

7. False – there is a continuing duty on the prosecutor, for the duration of the criminal proceedings against the accused, to disclose material, which satisfies the test for disclosure (subject to public interest considerations).

CHAPTER 7

CRITICAL THINKING ACTIVITY 7.1

The Human Rights Act 1998 is sacrosanct in criminal justice. There are occasions where breaches can take place, and these are enshrined in legislation. For example, you can kill someone in certain circumstances, if you are so fearful that the person would have killed or seriously harmed you.

The cases you should have looked at often fall into certain categories:

- ignorance of the law;

- laziness – not being bothered to do things correctly;

- intentional breaches designed to hide evidence;

- corrupt activities.

CRITICAL THINKING ACTIVITY 7.2

We operate under a due process model. Cases that often fail or are highlighted as a miscarriage of justice often fall within the crime control model. We recognise there are advantages of each model. You have been asked to consider a burglary, which is a serious crime, but does not attract great levels of emotion. Paedophiles, on the other hand, create an emotional response and therefore the emotion can take over our decision making.

You can supplement any other crime and see the differences, criminal damage versus terrorist activities as an example. Take some time and have a look at the 'trolley dilemma' (University of Exeter, 2020) in the context of decision making and then consider this against crime control.

REFLECTIVE PRACTICE 7.1

Looking at the court listings you can often see how a case progresses. You should see some of the language used that indicates why the case is progressing and start to pick up some of the themes.

If you have had the chance to visit a court, you should have been able to see the process. They are formal, which you would expect. There are significant differences between the magistrates' and Crown Court, both in terms of cases but also the behaviour and dress code. There is a formality at the Crown Court where the barristers wear wigs and gowns. What you should see in both courts is that there is a formality, including standing up when the magistrate or judge enters the court as a matter of respect. The process also dictates who speaks and when, how they address the court and the expectations of the magistrate or the judge.

CRITICAL THINKING ACTIVITY 7.3

It can be argued that if the case had been heard under adversarial conditions, then due to its processes and procedures fewer failings in the process of the court would be likely with a fairer outcome and the decision being made by the jury rather than a single judge.

The case of Meredith Kercher was reported on a global scale. The press coverage was constant and yet there were still significant failings.

Think about the case, the failings and whether they could occur in the UK.

REFLECTIVE PRACTICE 7.3

Farquharson Guidelines (CPS, 2020) states that all prosecution advocates when considering a please bargain must consult with the victims an the families and ensure they understand the effects of any plea bargaining this should be the first point of any decision making. Secondly you should consider the offender and their character and previous convictions. For some additional reading, please have a look at the Attorney General's guidance: www. gov.uk/guidance/the-acceptance-of-pleas-and-the-prosecutors-role-in-the-sentencing-exercise as this provides greater depth and explanation.

CHECK YOUR KNOWLEDGE

1. Article 6, Right to a fair trial 1. In the determination of their civil rights and obligations or of any criminal charge against them, everyone is entitled to a fair and public hearing within a reasonable time by an independent and impartial tribunal established by law.

2. A summary offence is categorised as one of the least serious offences. These types of offences can only be tried in the Magistrates' Court.

3. The difference is the second module prioritises the interests of the individual not of the state.

4. Plea bargaining is a tool that can be used to reduce the amount of court time utilised for a case and is used to ensure a guilty plea to a lesser charge.

5. An unreliable confession can lead to a miscarriage of justice.

6. Yes. Expert witnesses can be useful in a prosecution as they are able to offer expert opinion about a subject matter to assist the court or jury in concluding if the evidence before them is correct.

CHAPTER 8

CHECK YOUR KNOWLEDGE

1. Three to five years

2. Victims

3. Workshops – including educational programmes; anger management courses; social interaction courses; youth workers/activities (gyms/mechanics); unpaid work – working within the voluntary sector; time management courses

4. 1930s

5. Age

REFERENCES

Amir, M (1971) *Patterns of Forecable Rape*. Chicago: University of Chicago Press.

Animal Welfare Act 2006 [online] Available at: www.legislation.gov.uk/ukpga/2006/45/contents (accessed 6 October 2022).

Anti-social Behaviour, Crime and Policing Act 2014 [online] Available at: www.legislation.gov.uk/ukpga/2014/12/contents/enacted (accessed 6 October 2022).

Association of Chief Police Officers (ACPO) (2012) *Guidance on the Safer Detention and Handling of Persons in Police Custody*. NPIA. [online] Available at: https://assets.publishing.service.gov.uk/government/uploads/system/uploads/attachment_data/file/117555/safer-detention-guidance-2012.pdf (accessed 6 October 2022).

Attorney General's Office (2012) *Guidance: The Acceptance of Pleas and the Prosecutor's Role in the Sentencing Exercise*. [online] Available at: www.gov.uk/guidance/the-acceptance-of-pleas-and-the-prosecutors-role-in-the-sentencing-exercise (accessed 6 October 2022).

Attorney General's Office (2020) *Attorney General's Guidelines on Disclosure for Investigators, Prosecutors and Defence Practitioners*. [online] Available at: https://assets.publishing.service.gov.uk/government/uploads/system/uploads/attachment_data/file/946082/Attorney_General_s_Guidelines_2020_FINAL_Effective_31Dec2020.pdf (accessed 15 November 2022).

Attorney General's Office (2022) *Attorney General's Guidelines on Disclosure*. [online] Available at: https://assets.publishing.service.gov.uk/government/uploads/system/uploads/attachment_data/file/1078194/AG_Guidelines_2022_Revision_Publication_Copy.pdf (accessed 6 October 2022).

Bail Act 1976 [online] Available at: www.legislation.gov.uk/ukpga/1976/63/contents (accessed 6 October 2022).

Baird, V (2021) *Annual Report of the Victims' Commissioner 2020 to 2021*. [online] Available at: https://victimscommissioner.org.uk/document/annual-report-of-the-victims-commissioner-2020-to-2021 (accessed 6 October 2022).

Boardman, V (2015) EWCA Crim 175.

Case, S, Johnson, P, Manlow, D, Smith, R, Williams, K, Samota, N and Ugwudike, P (2017) *Criminology*. New York: Oxford University Press.

Children Act 2004 [online] Available at: www.legislation.gov.uk/ukpga/2004/31/contents (accessed 6 October 2022).

College of Policing (2013) *Code of Ethics*. [online] Available at: www.college.police.uk/ethics/code-of-ethics (accessed 6 October 2022).

College of Policing (2014) *Investigative Interviewing*. [online] Available at: www.college.police.uk/app/investigation/investigative-interviewing/investigative-interviewing   (accessed 11 October 2022)

College of Policing (2021) *Investigation Process – Material*. [online] Available at: www.college.police.uk/app/investigation/investigation-process#material (accessed 6 October 2022).

Courts and Tribunals Judiciary (2012) *Structure of the Courts and Tribunals System*. [online] Available at: www.judiciary.uk/structure-of-courts-and-tribunals-system/ (accessed 15 November 2022).

Crime and Disorder Act 1998 [online] Available at: www.legislation.gov.uk/ukpga/1998/37/contents (accessed 6 October 2022).

Criminal Justice Act 1998 www.legislation.gov.uk/ukpga/1988/33/contents (accessed 11 November 2022).

Criminal Justice Act 2003 [online] Available at: www.legislation.gov.uk/ukpga/2003/44/contents (accessed 6 October 2022).

Criminal Justice Act 2003 (Conditional Cautions: Code of Practice) Order 2013 [online] Available at: www.legislation.gov.uk/uksi/2013/801/contents/made (accessed 6 October 2022).

Criminal Justice and Immigration Act 2008 [online] Available at: www.legislation.gov.uk/ukpga/2008/4/contents (accessed 6 October 2022).

Criminal Justice and Police Act 2001 [online] Available at: www.legislation.gov.uk/ukpga/2001/16/contents (accessed 6 October 2022).

Criminal Justice and Public Order Act 1994 [online] Available at: www.legislation.gov.uk/ukpga/1994/33/contents (accessed 6 October 2022).

Criminal Law Act 1967 [online] Available at: www.legislation.gov.uk/ukpga/1967/58/section/3 (accessed 6 October 2022).

Criminal Procedure and Investigations Act 1996 [online] Available at: www.legislation.gov.uk/ukpga/1996/25/section/23 (accessed 6 October 2022).

Criminal Procedure and Investigations Act 1996. Section 23(1) – Code of Practice. [online] Available at: www.legislation.gov.uk/ukpga/1996/25/section/23 (accessed 6 October 2022).

Criminal Procedure Rules 2005 [online] Available at: www.legislation.gov.uk/uksi/2005/384/contents/made (accessed 6 October 2022).

Criminal Procedure Rules 2020 [online] Available at: www.legislation.gov.uk/uksi/2020/759/contents/made (accessed 6 October 2022).

Crown Prosecution Service (CPS) (2013a) *Director's Guidance on Adult Conditional Cautions* (7th ed). London: CPS.

Crown Prosecution Service (CPS) (2013b) *Director's Guidance on Youth Conditional Cautions*. London: CPS.

Crown Prosecution Service (CPS) (2018) *The Code for Crown Prosecution*. [online] Available at: www.cps.gov.uk/publication/code-crown-prosecutors (acessed 3 November 2022).

Crown Prosecution Service (CPS) (2020) *Farquharson Guidelines: Role of Prosecuting Advocates*. London: CPS. [online] Available at: www.cps.gov.uk/legal-guidance/farquharson-guidelines-role-prosecuting-advocates (accessed 6 October 2022).

Crown Prosecution Service (CPS) (2022) *Disclosure Manual: Chapter 1 – Introduction*. [online] Available at: www.cps.gov.uk/legal-guidance/disclosure-manual-chapter-1-introduction (accessed 6 October 2022).

DS and TS [2015] EWCA Crim 662.

Durisin, E and van der Meulen, E (2021) The Perfect Victim: 'Young Girls', Domestic Trafficking, and Anti-Prostitution Politics in Canada. *Anti-Trafficking Review*, 16: 145–9.

Equality Act 2010 [online] Available at: www.legislation.gov.uk/ukpga/2010/15/contents (accessed 6 October 2022).

European Convention on Human Rights (2010) [online] Available at: www.echr.coe.int/documents/convention_eng.pdf (accessed 6 October 2022).

Glen, S (2016) *Charging and Out of Court Disposals: A National Strategy 2017–2021*. [online] Available at: www.npcc.police.uk/Publication/Charging%20and%20Out%20 of%20Court%20Disposals%20A%20National%20Strategy.pdf (accessed 6 October 2022).

Glueck, S (1937) *Later Criminal Careers*. Oxford: Oxford University Press.

Gov.Scot (2015) *What Works to Reduce Reoffending: A Summary of the Evidence*. [online] Available at: www.gov.scot/publications/works-reduce-reoffending-summary-evidence/ pages/9 (accessed 6 October 2022).

Gov.uk (2002) *Changing Risk Behaviours and Promoting Cognitive Health in Older Adults*. [online] Available at: www.gov.uk/government/publications/changing-risk-behaviours-and-promoting-cognitive-health-in-older-adults (accessed 3 November 2022).

Gov.uk (2019) *New Rights for Victims of Crime*. [online] Available at: www.gov.uk/governm ent/news/new-rights-for-victims-of-crime (accessed 11 October 2022).

Gov.uk (2022) Criminal Procedure and Investigations Act 1996 (Section 23(1)) Code of Practice Revised in Accordance with Section 25(4) of the Criminal Proceudre and Investigations Act. [online] Available at: https://assets.publishing.service.gov.uk/governm ent/uploads/system/uploads/attachment_data/file/447967/code-of-practice-approved. pdf (accessed 11 October 2022).

Guardian (2022) Priti Patel Lifts Restrictions on Police Stop and Search Powers. [online] Available at: www.theguardian.com/law/2022/may/16/restrictions-on-police-stop-and-sea rch-powers-permanently-lifted (accessed 6 October 2022).

Home Office (2012) Police and Criminal Evidence Act 1984 – Code G. [online] Available at: https://assets.publishing.service.gov.uk/government/uploads/system/uploads/atta chment_data/file/903814/pace-code-g-2012.pdf (accessed 6 October 2022).

Home Office (2014) Police and Criminal Evidence Act 1984 (PACE) – Code A. [online] Available at: https://assets.publishing.service.gov.uk/government/uploads/system/uplo ads/attachment_data/file/384122/PaceCodeAWeb.pdf (accessed 6 October 2022).

Home Office (2015) Police and Criminal Evidence Act 1984 (PACE) – Code H. [online] Available at: https://assets.publishing.service.gov.uk/government/uploads/system/uplo ads/attachment_data/file/571728/57604_PACE_Code_H_2016_Print.pdf   (accessed 6 October 2022).

Horwell, R (2017) *Mouncher Investigation Report*. [online] Available at: https://assets.pub lishing.service.gov.uk/government/uploads/system/uploads/attachment_data/file/629 725/mouncher_report_web_accessible_july_2017.pdf (accessed 6 October 2022).

Howarth v Commissioner of Police of the Metropolis [2011] EWHC 2818 (Admin).

Human Rights Act 1998 [online] Available at: www.legislation.gov.uk/ukpga/1998/42/contents (accessed 6 October 2022).

Independent Police Complaints Commission (IPCC) (2016) *Investigation Arising from Operation Mayan into the Conduct of Detective Superintendent Stephen Fulcher*. London: Stationary Office.

Investigatory Powers Act 2016 [online] Available at: www.legislation.gov.uk/ukpga/2016/25/contents/enacted (accessed 6 October 2022).

Legal Aid, Sentencing and Punishment of Offenders Act (LASPO) 2012 [online] Available at: www.legislation.gov.uk/ukpga/2012/10/contents/enacted (accessed 6 October 2022).

Licensing Act 2003 [online] Available at: www.legislation.gov.uk/ukpga/2003/17/contents (accessed 6 October 2022).

Lumsden, K (2017) 'It's a Profession, It Isn't a Job': Police Officers' Views on the Professionalisation of Policing in England. *Sociological Research Online*, 22(3): 4–20.

Magistrates' Courts Act 1980 [online] Available at: www.legislation.gov.uk/ukpga/1980/43/contents (accessed 6 October 2022).

Macphearson, W (1999) *The Stephen Lawrence Inquiry: Report of an Inquiry by Sir William Macpheson of Cluny*. [online] Available at: https://assets.publishing.service. gov.uk/government/uploads/system/uploads/attachment_data/file/277111/4262.pdf (accessed 3 November 2022).

Maruna, S and King, A K (2009) Once a Criminal, Always a Criminal? 'Redeemability' and the Psychology of Punitive Public Attitudes. *European Journal on Criminal Policy and Research*, 15(1): 7–24.

Mendelsohn, B (1976) Victimology and Contemporary Society's Trends. *Victimology*, 1(1): 8–28.

Metropolitan Police Act 1829 [online] Available at: www.legislation.gov.uk/ukpga/Geo4/10/44/contents (accessed 6 October 2022).

Misuse of Drugs Act 1971 [online] Available at: www.legislation.gov.uk/ukpga/1971/38/contents (accessed 6 October 2022).

Newman. T (2005) *Handbook of Policing*. Abingdon: Willan Publishing.

Neyroud, P and Slothower, M (2015) Wielding the Sword of Damocles: The Challenges and Opportunities in Reforming Police Out-of-Court Disposals in England and Wales. In Wasik, M and Santatzoglou, S (eds) *The Management of Change in Criminal Justice* (pp 275–92). London: Palgrave Macmillan.

Offences against the Person Act 1861 [online] Available at: www.legislation.gov.uk/ukpga/Vict/24-25/100/contents (accessed 6 October 2022).

Ormerod, D (2003) Improving the Disclosure Regime. *International Journal of Evidence & Proof*, 7(2): 102–29.

Packer, H L (1964) Two Models of the Criminal Process. *University of Pennsylvania Law Review*, 113: 1.

Police Act 1996 [online] Available at: www.legislation.gov.uk/ukpga/1996/16/section/6AZA (accessed 6 October 2022).

Police and Criminal Evidence Act 1984 [online] Available at: www.legislation.gov.uk/ukpga/1984/60/contents (accessed 6 October 2022).

Police, Crime, Sentencing and Courts Act 2022 [online] Available at: www.legislation.gov.uk/ukpga/2022/32/contents (accessed 6 October 2022).

Police and Criminal Evidence Act 1984 [online] Available at: www.legislation.gov.uk/ukpga/1984/60/contents (accessed 6 October 2022).

Police Professional (2014) Offenders Face Consequences as Cautions Scrapped. *Police Professional*, 6 November, p 7.

Police Reform Act 2002 [online] Available at: www.legislation.gov.uk/ukpga/2002/30/section/12 (accessed 6 October 2022).

Proceeds of Crime Act 2002 [online] Available at: www.legislation.gov.uk/ukpga/2002/29/contents (accessed 6 October 2022).

Psychoactive Substances Act 2016 [online] Available at: www.legislation.gov.uk/ukpga/2016/2/contents/enacted (accessed 6 October 2022).

Public Order Act 1986 [online] Available at: www.legislation.gov.uk/ukpga/1986/64 (accessed 6 October 2022).

R v Allan [2016] Unreported Croyden Crown Court.

R v Fulling [1987] 2 All ER 65.

R v Goodyear [2005] EWCA Crim 888.

R v Hanson [2005] QEWCA Crim 824.

R v Howell (Errol) [1982] Q.B. 416.

R v Olu, Wilson and Brooks [2010] EWCA Crim 2975, [2011] 1 Cr. App. R. 33 [42]–[44].

R v R and Others [2015] EWCA Crim (1941).

R v Turnbull [1976] Cr App R 132.

Regulation of Investigatory Powers Act 2000 [online] Available at: www.legislation.gov.uk/ukpga/2000/23/contents (accessed 6 October 2022).

Reichel, P (2017) Comparative Criminal Justice Systems, 7th edition. Upper Saddle River, NJ: Pearson.

Restorative Justice Council (2016) Restorative Justice and Policing – What You Need to Know. [online] Available at: https://restorativejustice.org.uk/sites/default/files/resources/files/rjc-policeandrj-5digi.pdf (accessed 6 October 2022).

Restorative Justice Council (2022) Home Page. [online] Available at: https://restorativejustice.org.uk (accessed 6 October 2022).

Scarman, L G (1986) The Scarman Report: The Brixton Disorders 10–12 April 1981. Report of an Inquiry. London: Penguin.

Sentencing Council (2016) Sentencing – Allocation. [online] Available at: www.sentencingcouncil.org.uk/overarching-guides/magistrates-court/item/allocation (accessed 6 October 2022).

Serious Organised Crime and Police Act 2005 [online] Available at: www.legislation.gov.uk/ukpga/2005/15/contents (accessed 6 October 2022).

Stainton, I and Ewin, R (2022) *Criminal Investigation*. St Albans: Critical Publishing.

Stanier, I (2016) Enhancing Intelligence-Led Policing: Law Enforcement's Big Data Revolution. In Bunnik, A, Cawley, A, Mulqueen, M and Zwitter, A (eds) *Big Data Challenges* (pp 97–113). London: Palgrave Macmillan.

Terrorism Act 2000 [online] Available at: www.legislation.gov.uk/ukpga/2000/11/contents (accessed 6 October 2022).

Theobald, D and Farrington, D P (2014) Onset of Offending. In Bruinsma, G. and Weisburd, D (eds) *Encyclopedia of Criminology and Criminal Justice*. New York: Springer.

United Nations (1985) *1985 United Nations Declaration of Basic Principles of Justice for Victims of Crime and Abuse of Power*. [online] Available at: www.unicef-irc.org/portfolios/documents/472_un-declaration-crime.htm#:~:text=%22Victims%22%20means%20persons%20who%2C%20individually%20or%20collectively%2C%20have,including%20those%20laws%20proscribing%20criminal%20abuse%20of%20power   (accessed   11 November 2022).

University of Exeter (2020) Trolley Dilemma: When It's Acceptable to Sacrifice One Person to Save Others Is Informed by Culture. *Phys.org*. [online] Available at: https://phys.org/news/2020-01-trolley-dilemma-sacrifice-person-culture.html#:~:text=The%20%22Trolley%20Dilemma%27%20is%20an%20ethical%20thought%20experiment,in%20the%20train%20yard%2C%20next%20to%20a%20lever (accessed 3 November 2022).

Vomfell, L and Stewart, N (2021) Officer Bias, Over-Patrolling and Ethnic Disparities in Stop and Search. *Nature Human Behaviour*, 5(5): 566–75.

Von Hentig, H (1948) *The Criminal and His Victim: Studies in the Sociobiology of Crime*. New Haven, CT: Yale University Press.

Walsh, D W and Bull, R (2010) Interviewing Suspects of Fraud: An In-Depth Analysis of Interviewing Skills. *Journal of Psychiatry and Law*, 38(1–2): 99–135.

Walsh, D W and Milne, R (2008) Keeping the PEACE? A Study of Investigative Interviewing Practices in the Public Sector. *Legal and Criminological Psychology*, 13(1): 39–57.

INDEX

Page numbers in **bold** and *italics* denote tables and figures, repectively.

Printed in the United States
by Baker & Taylor Publisher Services

Printed in the United States
by Baker & Taylor Publisher Services